LIFE SKILLS FOR TEENS UNLOCKED

MASTER INDEPENDENT LIVING BY LEARNING TO MANAGE MONEY, SHARPEN COOKING ABILITIES, UNCOVER CLEANING HACKS, DIVE INTO YOUR SELF-DISCOVERY & DEVELOPMENT, AND MUCH MORE

JOY PACK

CONTENTS

INTRODUCTION

Being a teen today is tough! You deal with stuff teens have faced for thousands of years, plus some new challenges this world has never seen before. You need a good guide, a playbook, and a mentor to help you figure out how to handle it all and grow up strong.

Fun fact: did you know your brain keeps growing until you're around 25? So, no rush—you've got time to figure things out! The teenage years, from puberty to adulthood, are called adolescence.

This book is your go-to guide, both for now and as you grow older. Each chapter is a guided step on your journey. Dive into what catches your eye now, and come back later to explore more about becoming your amazing future self!

Hi, I'm Joy! I'm a fun and spirited woman who isn't afraid to laugh at my awkward adolescence. I try to see life clearly and keep growing and rediscovering who I am. Listen up, fam: I still rock my millennial-style skinny jeans and side part, but I've become confident and capable and am good at this whole "adulting" thing.

Let's rewind to my awkward teen years, where the toughest decision was whether to stick to my trusty Graphic-T and jeans or go all out with denim-on-denim. I was just a young, awkward girl trying to find my place and impress my friends.

In some moments, I felt like I was on top of the world, and in others, I felt like a nervous wreck. Ever had those days when a small choice felt like it would change your life forever? Yeah, me too. But spoiler alert: it's usually just a regular Tuesday.

I've only lived in the United States of America, mostly in Arizona and New England. This book's terms and details are written mainly in American English language, spelling, culture and terms. However, I've taken special care to include specific UK and Canada tidbits, too—because growing up is a global adventure!

Throughout this book, you'll find cool extras titled "***Tip & Action***." They look like this:

Tip & Action: *Take a moment to pull out a notebook, pen, pencil, or whatever means works best for you (notebook, journal, tablet, smartphone, computer). Get ready to track what you are thinking and learning, and the answers to prompts from the **Tip & Action** steps. Feel free to mark up in the book too!*

Go visit my site at creatingourjoy.com *to see my work pages, guides, blog posts, links and more to help you dive deeper into the skills found in this book!*

Some are quick tips, like finding a YouTube video, and others are more hands-on. As you try them out, you'll be amazed at how much you can learn and grow!

Heads up! Lots of tips in this book involve using the internet, so chat with your folks about staying safe online. Always keep online safety in mind and set good boundaries when browsing or using apps. If you prefer offline learning, keep a list of what you want to dive into and then head to your local library or bookshop and chat with other folks.

This book's here to share info and help you learn, but it's not professional advice. Think of it like advice from a cool aunt! Do your own research and talk to pros before making big decisions.

Congrats on starting this journey! You're already ahead of the game, so keep reading and trying new things. Be patient with yourself as you learn new skills and celebrate your progress.

If you struggle with issues like being neurodivergent or having ADHD or dyslexia, there are specific strategies and adaptations you can find to cater to your needs and help you succeed. Check out my website for a compilation of resources and linked videos for more in-depth learning.

This book has two sections: first, fun "household skills" and "life-hacks" for everyone! It's a quick start to new skills and info. The second section leads you through a deeper dive into self-discovery and growth.

So, let's begin!

There are QR Codes throughout the book so that if you have a paper version, you can easily access the fun videos or helpful resources I reference. In the e-book there are links within the text explanation. If there is an expired or wrong link you can just go to my website and follow the walkthrough of links posted there. These links and QR codes will appear again at the very end of the book for quick reference.

Here are the QR codes I will refer to throughout the book to my website CreatingOurJoy.com & my Amazon author page

MY WEBSITE	MY AMAZON
CreatingOurJoy.com	Author Site

CHAPTER ONE
MASTERING SKILLS FOR INSIDE THE HOME

Hey there, fearless teen! Opening up a book like this can stir up all sorts of feelings. But guess what? I'm here, to make learning and growing feel like an epic adventure!

Think about it: how do you take care of the things you love? How do you keep the good stuff shining bright and kick the ick to the curb? Cheers to diving into this chapter—it's your first step on an awesome journey!

Before you dive into cleaning, fixing, or sprucing things up, make sure you've got the right tools, gear, and a plan. No need to be a plumbing pro like Mario from The Super Mario Bros. Movie, but knowing a few home upkeep basics can save you time, cash, and earn you some serious respect.

Here are some common protective equipment and tools you might need:

Protective Equipment:

- Gloves: Protect your hands from chemicals, dirt, and sharp objects.
- Goggles: Keep your eyes safe from dust, debris, and chemicals.
- Masks: Prevent inhaling dust, fumes, or mold.
- Ear Protection: Use earplugs or earmuffs when using loud tools.
- Closed-Toe Shoes: Protect your feet from heavy or sharp objects.

Tools for Cleaning:

- Broom and Dustpan: For sweeping floors.
- Mop and Bucket: For cleaning floors with water and soap.
- Vacuum Cleaner: For cleaning carpets and rugs.
- Sponges and Scrub Brushes: For scrubbing surfaces.
- Cleaning Cloths: For wiping surfaces.

- Spray Bottles: For applying cleaning solutions.
- Trash Bags: For collecting garbage and debris.

Tools for Home Maintenance:

- Screwdrivers: For tightening or loosening screws.
- Flathead Screwdrivers: flat, straight tip.
- Phillips Screwdrivers: pointed, cross-shaped
- Hammer: For driving nails into surfaces.
- Pliers: For gripping and bending objects.
- Wrenches: For turning nuts and bolts.
- Tape Measure: For measuring lengths and distances.
- Level: For making sure surfaces are straight.
- Utility Knife: For cutting materials.
- Ladder: For reaching high places.
- Torch or Lighter: To form material or start a stove or candles.

Tools for Repairs:

- Drill and Drill Bits: For making holes and driving screws.
- Saw: For cutting wood or metal.
- Stud Finder (or strong magnet): For locating studs in walls.
- Caulking Gun: For applying caulk to seal gaps.
- Patch Kits: For repairing holes in walls.

Always remember to follow safety instructions and ask for help if you're unsure about something. Stay safe, and have fun with your projects!

CARE & CLEANING

Keeping your space neat and tidy isn't just about appearances—it's about feeling good and staying healthy. Plus, it shows that you care about yourself and others, including your furry pals! Taking care of your stuff and tidying up after yourself, especially when you're borrowing or visiting, earns major brownie points with folks.

When you stay on top of cleaning and maintenance, your home becomes a peaceful oasis. No more last-minute scrambles to tidy up before guests arrive! Let's aim for that sweet spot between a chaotic mess and a show home no one actually lives in.

__Tip & Action:__ Now, don't get stuck scrolling through videos, but watch the first 30 seconds of this dramatic YouTube video (Chris Fleming, 2015, COMPANY IS COMING), it's that classic freak out some moms have to get the house spotless before company comes.

Regular cleaning isn't just about keeping things looking nice—it's about keeping you healthy, too! Dust can build up over time, causing allergies and annoying symptoms like sneezing and watery eyes. Yuck! When you dust, use a damp cloth or a special dusting cloth to trap the dust and stop it from flying around. Remove dust from surfaces like shelves, tables, and electronics. Work from top to bottom to prevent dust from settling on already cleaned areas. Then, when you use a vacuum, make sure to vacuum in multiple directions to get more dirt and dust out.

If you've got chores at home, make sure to do them right. Chat with your family about how they like things done. For example, do you move chairs to sweep under the table? How about getting those hard-to-reach spots under the fridge and stove? Knowing the drill helps you do a stellar job!

Doing laundry can be a breeze if you follow a few simple steps. First off, always remember to check your pockets before tossing clothes in the hamper. No one wants a surprise in the washing machine! When it's time to do the wash, sort your clothes by color and fabric type to keep everything looking fresh. You want to wash like colors, usually in 3 groups, whites, light colors, dark colors. You want to make sure the colors don't bleed and affect each other, like a new red towel or jeans could make your white towels come out looking like a tie dye flag!

Next, use the right amount of detergent and pick the correct settings on the washing machine for best results. Then hang to dry or if putting them into the dryer make sure to clean the lint fuzz out, and proceed with the appropriate settings there too.

Once your clothes are clean and dry, don't forget to fold them and put them away. It helps to have three hampers: one for dirty clothes, one for clean ones, and one for those in-between pieces. This way, you can stay organized and avoid clutter even when you feel too busy or unmotivated to fully put your laundry away.

If you're in a rush and your clothes need a quick refresh, give them a spritz with water or a mix of water and essential oils, like citrus or floral scents. Then, toss them in the dryer or hang them up flat. They'll come out smelling nice and looking wrinkle-free, ready for whatever the day brings!

Tip & Action: *Check out my site creatingourjoy.com for more cleaning hacks, money and energy saving guides, and ways to organize and discuss clearing and chore standards in your home.*

An organized space isn't just about looks—it's about boosting productivity and lowering stress levels, too! Websites like apart-menttherapy.com have awesome tips for getting your home in order. Plus, apps like Tody, FlyLadyPlus, and Sweepy can help you stay on track, especially when things feel overwhelming.

Organizing your stuff, both in real life and on your devices, makes life easier. Keep your computer files in folders with clear labels and back them up regularly. We will dive more into technical skills in a bit. For physical files, use containers like bins or drawers, and don't forget to label everything! Important documents, like passports and birth certificates, should be kept safe, and it's smart to have copies in different places just in case. Once I moved out of my parents, I kept a copy of my birth certificate at my moms house too in case there was a fire or theft at my place.

Some documents, like birth certificates and life insurance policies, are keepers forever. Others have an expiration date—think tax docs for 7 years and regular bills for just a month. And remember, shred any docs with personal info before tossing them out to keep your privacy intact.

Knowing how to care for and repair your belongings can save you time and money. Learning basic sewing skills can help you fix or alter clothes. You'll need tools like scissors, needles, thread, and fabric patches. For thick materials like jeans, use a thicker needle and thread. Common repairs include sewing on a button or fixing a rip. You can learn these skills from classes, online videos, or a friend or neighbor who knows how to sew.

Keeping pests under control is important for cleanliness and sanity. Common pests include ants, cockroaches, mice, and spiders. Keep your home clean and seal food to prevent pests from coming in. Check and clean areas where pests might gather. Seal cracks and drafts in doors and windows to keep pests out and save on heating and cooling costs.

Safety first! Knowing about local pests can also help you stay safe. Like, in Arizona, it's good to know basic first aid for bites and stings from rattlesnakes, spiders, and scorpions. Some can be treated at home, but others need emergency medical attention.

Taking care of your belongings helps them last longer. Keep things clean and maintained with the right tools and solutions. For example, use a leather conditioner for your couch and lemon essential oil for squeaky hinges.

Keeping your space clean and organized helps you feel calm and in control. My family has a motto: "A place for everything, and everything in its place." Another version is "Outer order, inner calm."

Leave things better than you found them.

This applies to everything, from cleaning up the kitchen after cooking to picking up trash on a hike. It even applies to how you leave yourself and other humans feeling at the end of an interaction! Love and respect is key!

Treat other people's stuff and spaces with care, and they'll be more likely to trust you and let you borrow again. Whether you're into rock, hip-hop, or anything in between, belonging starts with respect. And hey, when you borrow something, give it back in better shape than you found it. Clean up after yourself and show gratitude—it's the adulting way!

Tip & Action: *Treat anything you borrow as well and precisely as the owner does, and then at least a little better.*

Clean & Fresh, Hygiene

Ah, the wonderful world of puberty—the time when body odor becomes a whole new level of funky! Body odor happens when sweat mixes with bacteria, and let's just say it's not the most pleasant combo.

Enter the lymphatic system: this amazing network of vessels and organs plays a huge role in sweating and body odor. Most of the action goes down in your armpits and groin, where most lymph nodes hang out. Less airflow in these areas means more odor, so good hygiene is key.

Forget harsh chemicals – we're talking natural, crunchy stuff like apple cider vinegar (ACV). Baking soda, also known as bicarbonate of soda, is another helpful and cheap option for many different uses in health and grooming! You could write a whole book on the uses of vinegar (white, apple, and others) and baking soda in health, cleaning, and more!

Tip & Action: Vinegar, baking soda, borax, bleach & essential oils (like tea tree, lavender & peppermint) are all powerhouses for cleaning, grooming, and hygiene. You don't need the expensive bottles and toxic chemical mixes.

Anytime you are working with plant/essential oils, become familiar with their benefits, risks, portions to use, and the carrier oils (like coconut or castor) to mix it with.

For ACV wash put it in a spray bottle with 1 part ACV and 1 part water, and voila! You've got a magical spray that keeps bacteria at bay and leaves you smelling fresh as a daisy. Just add to body soap or spray right on your body in the shower, scrub and rub, and rinse! Side note, when you bar-b-que or smoke meat that ACV mixture also works really well, just spraying it on the cuts of meat throughout the process helps to keep it moist!

For baking soda you can add ¼ cup to a warm bath and soak for up to 40 minutes to relieve itching, irritation, infections, and detox. This may help with a range of conditions such as eczema. You can also add it to your facial cleanser for mild exfoliation or make a paste with 3 parts baking soda and 1 part water. This mixture can be applied to pesky pimple spots to help cleanse, exfoliate, and draw out infections.

Afraid of that sweet symphony of puberty we just mentioned?—the time when body odor becomes a full-blown concert!—fear not, my friends, for with a little know-how and some TLC, we can tame even the wildest smells.

Let's start with the basics: what you put in your body affects what comes out. Yup, it's true—eating clean and staying hydrated can help keep those funky odors at bay. So say goodbye to processed junk and hello hydration!

You also want to ensure your clothes are clean, washed thoroughly, and dried. You want the environments you are in to be cleaned regularly. Have your room, bathroom, and vehicle clear of trash and free of smelly clothes, animal issues, or old foods.

Specifically for armpit odors and health, you want to clean, dry, and use healthy products that work best for you. Products with specific antibacterial properties, like lavender, eucalyptus, peppermint, and tea tree oils, can help cut through the bacteria and protect your skin.

I remember my own puberty pit predicament like it was yesterday. Sweaty circles under my arms? Check. But as I learned more about my body and how to take care of it, those embarrassing moments became a thing of the past. I learned to wear looser shirts of black or lighter colors. Tight gray shirts are not where they are when you have an active lymphatic system!

Ah, the nitty-gritty of groin hygiene! Let's dive into keeping your private parts squeaky clean and smelling like their natural, beautiful musk.

For all genders, getting in there and giving everything a good scrub-down is key. If you're lucky enough to have a removable shower head, that's your golden ticket for a direct rinse and thorough cleaning. Rinse from front to back and then between from the back for a thorough clean.

Now, let's talk specifics. We will discuss Male and Female anatomy in more detail later, but to get the idea… Guys, it's all about getting between and under every nook and cranny of your genitals. Give 'em a good scrub with soap, just like you do with the rest of your body. And remember, cleanliness is key, so don't forget about your backdoor – give it a thorough scrub and rinse for good measure.

Girls, your lady parts deserve some extra TLC. Avoid using products not meant for your delicate parts – your vagina and vulva have their own beautiful pH balance that you don't want to mess with. Stick to gentle cleansers for your outer labia and groin area, and make sure to rinse thoroughly.

Now, the post-shower routine – it's like the cherry on top of a clean sundae! Let's wrap things up with some final touches to keep you feeling fresh and fabulous.

After you've rinsed off, it's time to dry off. But here's the trick: use separate towels for your face/head and body. Trust me, you don't want to be drying your face with the same towel you used on your backside! I like to keep it simple with a red towel for my head and a blue one for my body – easy to remember, right? "Red for head, blue for body."

Once you're all dry, it's time to pamper your skin. Slather on some good lotions or oils to keep everything feeling soft and moisturized. Your skin will thank you for it! After you shower, and possibly throughout the day, you may want to apply a good deodorant. It's great to start with something your family uses and then branch out to what you like and what works best over time. Finding what works best for you might take some trial and error, but trust me, it's worth it.

And hey, let's talk about those pesky bathroom moments. If you're having trouble getting your backside clean after a bathroom break, don't worry – you're not alone! Baby wipes are a game-changer for that extra clean feeling. Trust me, toilet paper alone just doesn't cut it most times; just don't flush them down the toilet. Keep wiping and folding and getting new wipes until you are all clean!

And if you're feeling fancy, you might even consider investing in a bidet. They're all the rage these days, especially since "the great toilet paper crisis of 2020." Plus, they're a more eco-friendly option that helps reduce paper waste.

Tip & Action: *When you have to poop and you want to hide the stench, you can use a before-you-go toilet spray. This can be purchased like the Poo-Pourri Toilet Spray or a DIY spray. A recipe I use is to take an empty spray bottle and mix water, alcohol, and essential oils. A recipe I have used over and over is 3 oz water, 1 tsp rubbing alcohol, and 30 drops of essential oils (I prefer peppermint and lemon for this spray). Then you just keep it by your toilet, and before you go, shake the bottle and spray it onto the water in the toilet bowl 3 times. You can also make it to go and add it to your travel hygiene bag (discussed in a moment) if you want.*

So there you have it – the finishing touches to your clean routine. With a little TLC and some handy tips, you'll be feeling fresh and fabulous every day!

Now, what about when you are out and about? Face and baby wipes are great for freshening up on the go! You can use one on your face and anywhere else, like your arms and chest. When you need a quick but deeper freshen-up, use one on your pits and another on your groin, then butt.

A quick wipe down and reapplication of your deodorant and a little spritz of your favorite smells can work wonders to keep you smelling and feeling clean and fresh. The key is to have clean and dry areas and have a hint of a good scent on top of that base. No need to stay in that classic Jr. High stage of just staying stinky and masking the stench with 10 pumps of a strong body spray.

Finally, the freshen-up bag – your secret weapon for staying fresh on the go! Let's put together the ultimate kit to keep you feeling so fresh and so clean, clean! No matter where life takes you!

First things first, choose a bag that fits your style and life. Whether it's a purse, backpack, fanny pack, or even just a pouch in your car, make sure it's something you can easily take with you wherever you go.

Now, let's stock it up! Here's what you'll need:

1. Face & Baby wipes: These little wonders are perfect for freshening up on the fly. Keep a small bunch in your bag for quick clean-ups anytime, anywhere.
2. Deodorant: A must-have for staying fresh all day long. Choose your favorite scent and make sure to reapply as needed throughout the day.
3. Toothbrush, toothpaste, floss, mouthwash: Keep your smile sparkling with a travel-size toothbrush, floss and toothpaste/mouthwash. A quick brush after meals can keep your breath fresh and your teeth clean.
4. Gum: For those moments when you need a quick breath freshener, throw in a pack of your favorite gum or mints.
5. Menstrual hygiene products: For those days when Aunt Flo comes to visit, make sure you're prepared with pads, tampons, or whatever you prefer.
6. Clean socks, underwear/knickers, and a shirt: You never know when you might need a quick change of clothes. Keep a spare pair set in your bag for emergencies.
7. Hair comb: for quick fixes to tidy your hair before an interview, date, or seeing relatives.
8. Hand sanitizer: to keep clean and reduce spread of germs and disease. I make my own recipe with 2 parts rubbing alcohol, 1 part aloe vera gel, and some essential oil drops like lavender.
9. Baggies: Keep something like Ziplocks or small trash bags handy for dirty clothes and rubbish (from every day trash to use tampons/pads if needed). You'll thank yourself later for keeping things neat and tidy.

Once you've assembled your freshen-up bag, don't forget to use it! Throw it in your main bag or keep it in your car so it's always ready when you need it. And remember to throw away any trash or dirty clothes once you get home – a clean bag is a happy bag!

With your freshen-up bag by your side, you'll be ready to tackle anything life throws your way with confidence and style. Stay fresh!

__Tip & Action:__ Put together a freshen-up bag, like the travel hygiene bag you would put in your suitcase on a trip. Make it personalized, however small or big you want, so you can bring it along and stay fresh.

Keeping your kicks and gear smelling fresh is crucial for both hygiene and comfort. Here are some pro tips to keep those odors at bay:

First off, make sure your gear has room to breathe. Store them in a well-ventilated area where they can dry out fully between uses. Consider setting up a designated spot outdoors, under cover, where they can air out naturally and avoid trapping moisture.

Next, pay attention to what you're wearing with your shoes. Opt for clean socks made from breathable materials like bamboo or wool to prevent bacteria buildup and odor transfer. Some folks even rotate between multiple pairs of shoes to let each pair air out properly between wears.

If you're battling stubborn odors, DIY odor-fighting sprays or sprinkles can be a game-changer. Mix up some rubbing alcohol with essential oils like tea tree or cinnamon to freshen up your footwear and equipment. And don't forget about baking soda—it's a natural deodorizer that works wonders for eliminating odors from stinky shoes. Just sprinkle it inside your shoes, let it sit overnight, and voila! Fresh kicks in the morning.

By incorporating these practices into your routine, you can keep your shoes and gear clean, dry, and smelling fresh. As you grow older, developing a solid hygiene routine with regular maintenance checks will keep you feeling and smelling your best.

Each part of your hygiene, cleaning, and life is slowly becoming, or already is, your full responsibility. Take charge of your schedule and develop a routine like:

- Brush my teeth every morning, after school, and at night (this is especially important for good looking teeth, and oral health which directly connects to many parts of the body!)

Brush my teeth & use mouthwash every morning
Brush my teeth after school/lunch
Brush & floss my teeth, then scrape my tongue every night

- Face skincare routine every night
- Fully clean my bathroom every Monday

All stuff put away, sweep & mop, scrub shower & toilet, wipe down mirror & counter & toilet, trash out

- Fully clean my room every Tuesday

Trash/dishes out, all stuff put away, vacuum, wipe down

- Do a load of laundry fully every Thursday

Wash pillowcases & towels every week

- Fully clean my car every Saturday

- Wash all bedding every other weekend

Take pride and ownership in your appearance and health. Figure out what routine works for you at this time.

HOME URGENCIES & EMERGENCIES

Fire Safety

You do not want to be trapped in a fire-safety or first-aid issue unprepared!

Tip & Action: DO NOT fall into a scrolling paralysis but, check out this classic clip (The Office, 2023, Fire Drill - The Office US) to get the vibe!

Fire safety is a skill that everyone should know because you never know when you might need it! Here are some key tips to keep in mind:

First off, make sure your home smoke detectors are in tip-top shape. Keep those batteries charged and test them regularly by pressing the test button. This checks both the battery power and the alarm function, so you can rest easy knowing they're ready to go if needed.

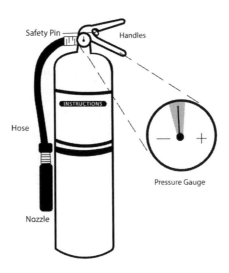

Safety Pin / Handles / Hose / INSTRUCTIONS / Nozzle / Pressure Gauge

Next, let's talk about fire extinguishers. These handy devices can be lifesavers in an emergency, so it's important to have them on hand and up-to-date. Check the location, accessibility, and status of your fire extinguishers at least once a year. Look for that good/green zone on the gauge to know if it's safe to use, and make sure the safety pin is in place and the spray nozzle is clear and clean. And don't forget to read the instruction label so you know exactly what to do in case of a fire!

By taking these simple steps, you can help keep yourself and your loved ones safe in case of a fire emergency.

Fire safety is a team effort, so be sure to work with your family to create a fire escape plan and know how to call emergency services if needed. Check out cool tools like the Prepared Hero Fire Blanket, which you can see in action on the 12 News YouTube channel in the video "Does It Work? Prepared Hero Fire Blanket." Find the safety tools that work best for you and get comfortable using them!

The American Red Cross in the US and firesafe.org.uk in the UK offer free fire safety tips to help keep you and your loved ones safe. Remember never to leave cooking or candles unattended, close bedroom doors at night to slow down smoke and fire, stay low if there's smoke, and be cautious with space heaters and electrical appliances. And don't forget to practice what to do if your clothes catch fire—stop, drop, and roll. Many local Fire Departments also offer free fire safety education programs that you can join to learn more.

Plumbing

Plumbing is like the lifeblood of your home—it's the system of pipes and fixtures that bring fresh water in and waste out. Think sinks, toilets, showers, and water heaters—they're all part of your plumbing setup.

Freshwater flows into your home through a water supply system, usually connected to a city's water source or an underground water system like a well or borehole. Then, when you're done with it, wastewater and sewage get whisked away by the drainage system, either to the sewer system or a septic tank.

But here's the thing: water leaks can be a real headache if they're not caught early. That's why it's super important to know where your home's water shut-off valve is and how to turn it off in case of a leak. Team up with your folks to locate it together and make sure you have the right tools on hand, just in case.

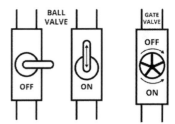

Common plumbing issues often come from the toilet. If you notice the toilet keeps filling and sounds like it's running, it's usually because the flapper/flush valve isn't sealing properly. Take a moment to lift the lid off your toilet tank and look inside. Flush the toilet and see how all the parts work together. It's basic yet interesting!

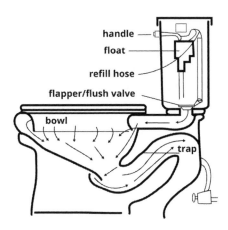

In a traditional toilet, the outer flush handle is connected to a bar, and a chain is hooked to the flush flapper. When you pull the handle, it releases water into the toilet, pushing the contents down the drain. There's also a floating ball that opens the fill valve when it lowers and closes it once the water is at the right level.

Often, I find that my toilet seat becomes loose. To fix it, I open the lid connection cover and use a flathead screwdriver to hold the bolt in place. Then, I tighten the wingnut from underneath.

EEk, the dreaded toilet clog—every plumber's rite of passage! Picture this: you're minding your business when suddenly, your toilet decides it's had enough and refuses to flush properly. Cue the plunger! A simple clog is often caused by something stuck in the drain, like a wad of toilet paper or a rogue toy that took a wrong turn. But fear not, young apprentice plumber, for with the mighty plunger in hand, you shall conquer this foe!

First things first, let's talk about toilet etiquette. Tampons, menstrual products, and anything that's not meant to go down the drain should never be flushed. Dispose of them in a waste bin to prevent pesky clogs and keep your plumbing happy.

Now, onto the main event: the plunger! Before you face off against the clog, it's time to practice your plunging technique. Make sure the toilet bowl is filled with enough water to cover the plunger cup. Then, place the plunger over the drain, ensuring a snug fit, and plunge away! Use controlled, steady pressure with an up-and-down motion for about 15 plunges. If the water starts to drain, victory is yours! If not, repeat the process until the clog surrenders.

But wait, what if the water level rises ominously? Don't panic! Seek assistance from a responsible adult before things get messy. And remember, after vanquishing the clog, rinse the plunger clean and store it in a dry, dignified manner.

Now, let's tackle another common plumbing nuisance: low water pressure. To fix this, clean faucet aerators (the little screen where the water comes out) and showerheads. Unscrew and remove the aerator or showerhead, check for buildup or debris, and rinse under running water.

When cleaning, it's cheap and effective to use common white or distilled vinegar, and it's a great tool to clear out debris and calcification. For a showerhead, fill a bag (like a gallon ziplock) with white vinegar, attach it to the showerhead, fully immerse it, and let it soak for about 30 minutes. Alternatively, you can soak towels in that vinegar, wrap them around the showerhead or tap, and leave them overnight. After soaking, scrub with an old toothbrush, dish brush, or sponge. Then, put everything back in place and run the water to rinse it out.

And what about those sneaky drain clogs that lurk beneath the surface? Fear not, for the hook method shall come to your rescue! Armed with a bent metal clothes hanger, crochet hook, or a handy tool like the "Hair Snake," you'll pull those pesky hairballs out of hiding and restore your drains to their former glory.

Remember, prevention is key! Install drain screens and sink stoppers to catch debris before it causes trouble, and laugh in the face of clogs as you conquer them like a seasoned plumbing pro.

Tip & **Action:** *Now, you know the drill: Don't get sidetracked with scrolling after you watch this but, check out this clip (Peacock, 2023, Zero-tolerance Phil is a monster,) and learn about the chore of unclogging the shower drain, sometimes it's just gotta be done, but see why prevention is key!*

Without question, taking initiative and addressing issues promptly is a superpower everyone should harness!

If something's bothering you, take care of it ASAP!

This can be anything! Like, the shower isn't draining well, the trash is full, the toilet paper is gone, or the squeaky door hinge drives you crazy. The energy it takes to harbor resentment, or the extra time you have to deal with a problem waiting for someone else to solve it is so avoidable. Just take responsibility and action and solve the immediate problem! Unclog the shower drain, replace the toilet paper, and put a backup close, or oil the hinge.

When it comes to group or relationship dynamics, communication is key. Having open discussions and setting clear boundaries ensures that everyone is on the same page and can work together harmoniously. So, if you find yourself in a sticky situation with your friends or loved ones, don't hesitate to speak up and find solutions together. After all, teamwork makes the dream work!

Electrical

Electricity is amazing and powers almost everything in our modern world, like lights, appliances, and gadgets. But how does it work? In simple terms, electricity is created by the movement of tiny particles called electrons. These electrons move through wires, creating a flow of electric current that we use to power things.

One important thing to know about in your home is the breaker box or fuse box. This is like the control center for your home's electricity. Inside the box are switches called circuit breakers, and sometimes there are fuses. These control the flow of electricity to different parts of your home. When the switches are on, electricity flows; when it's off, the electricity stops.

The box usually has labels to show which switch controls which part of your home. If you ever lose power in part of your home, this is one of the first places to check. Circuit breakers are designed to "trip" (switch off) if too much electricity flows through them, which helps prevent damage and fires.

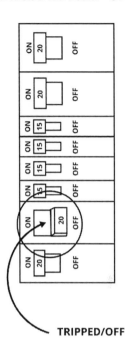

If a breaker trips, it will look different from the others because it will be switched off. To fix it, push the switch fully to the off position and then back on so it lines up with the others. Often it is helpful to have someone at the box and another person in the problem area to shout to, or be on the phone with, each other if the power is restored.

TRIPPED/OFF

Understanding GFI outlets and how they work is another important aspect of electrical safety in your home. These outlets are like the guardians of electricity, equipped with special features to keep you safe from ground faults. If something goes wrong and there's a ground fault, like if water gets into an outlet, the GFI outlet will detect it and shut off the power automatically, preventing electric shocks.

When a GFI outlet trips, it's like a warning sign that something isn't right. But don't worry! You can easily reset it by pressing the reset button located in the middle of the outlet. However, it's essential to investigate why the GFI tripped in the first place to prevent it from happening again. Maybe there's water where it shouldn't be, or an appliance is malfunctioning. Once you've addressed the issue, simply press the reset button, and you're good to go!

In addition to GFI outlets, it's important to understand what might cause breakers, fuses, or GFI outlets to trip. Overloading circuits with too many appliances or using faulty appliances can trigger them to trip. For example, running a blow-dryer and a space heater at the same time might overload the circuit and cause it to trip. If this happens, it's crucial to identify the cause and make adjustments before continuing to use electrical appliances.

And if the power goes out in your entire house, it might be due to a problem with the main breaker switch or an issue with the power company. In case of power outages, it's wise to be prepared with emergency supplies like flashlights, lanterns, and blankets to stay warm or cool depending on the weather. And remember, avoid opening your fridge and freezer unnecessarily to preserve your food and keep it from spoiling.

Understanding how your home's electrical system works and knowing how to troubleshoot common issues can help keep you safe and prepared for any electrical mishaps that may occur.

Weather

Understanding and preparing for local weather conditions is crucial for staying safe during emergencies. Different regions face unique weather challenges, so it's essential to know what to expect and how to respond. Whether it's tornadoes, earthquakes, flooding, hurricanes, or other severe weather events, being informed and prepared can make a significant difference.

In areas prone to tornadoes, it's important to have a plan in place for seeking shelter, such as a basement or an interior room on the lowest floor of a sturdy building. Earthquake-prone regions should have emergency kits with essentials like food, water, and first aid supplies, as well as secure furniture and heavy objects to prevent them from toppling during tremors.

For regions susceptible to flooding, understanding evacuation routes and having emergency supplies ready can be lifesaving. It's also crucial to stay informed about weather forecasts and warnings from local authorities to take appropriate action.

In Arizona, where I live, preparing for hot weather, monsoons, and haboobs requires specific precautions. Securing outdoor furniture and being aware of flood risks are essential steps to take before severe weather hits. Additionally, having emergency supplies like water, non-perishable food, and flashlights can help you weather the storm safely.

By staying informed, having a plan, and being prepared for local weather conditions, you can better protect yourself and your loved ones during emergencies. It's also a good idea to regularly review and update your emergency plans and supplies to ensure readiness at all times.

Water and Food Storage

Preparing an emergency supply of water and non-perishable food is essential for weathering tough times, whether due to natural disasters, financial difficulties, or other emergencies. Following guidelines from organizations like the World Health Organization and the CDC can help ensure you have enough resources to sustain yourself and your family during challenging situations.

For water storage, aim to have at least one gallon per person per day for drinking and sanitation purposes. It's recommended to store a two-week supply if possible. In case of sudden emergencies, filling your bathtub with water can provide an additional source, typically holding around 30 gallons. Water filters like LifeStraw can also be invaluable for purifying water from various sources.

When it comes to food supplies, start with enough to last for a week and gradually build up to two weeks or more. Ideally, aim for a three-month supply of non-perishable food items that don't require refrigeration or freezing. Canned goods, dried fruits, nuts, and long-term storage options like freeze-dried foods are excellent choices. Honey is an especially durable and nutritious option. Having a reliable can opener ensures you can access your food supplies when needed.

In addition to food and water, it's crucial to have a 72-hour kit or go-bag prepared for each member of your household. These kits should contain essentials like food, water, first aid supplies, medications, important documents, and clothing.

Regularly review and update your emergency supplies to ensure they remain adequate and effective over time. Websites like www.ready.gov/kit offer comprehensive lists of items to include in your emergency kit and provide valuable guidance for emergency preparedness.

Emergencies and Safety

We will review this again later on when we discuss mental health and other skills but I wanted to make sure and mention it here early too!

In any emergency, call the emergency number for help.

- **In the US & Canada, the emergency number is 911.** This number is used to contact police, fire, or medical services in case of an emergency.

- **In the UK, the emergency number is 999.** This number is used to contact the police, fire brigade, ambulance service, or other emergency services in case of an emergency.

The helper on the other end of the line should be well-trained and can walk you through the basics of most situations on the phone until other trained professionals are available in person to take over.

If you ever find yourself in a sticky situation that's not an emergency but you still need some help, don't fret! You can easily find the local non-emergency police numbers using Google or Siri. And if you're not sure which number to call, just dial 911 and let them know what's up. They can connect you to the right folks!

I had a wild encounter when my neighbor spotted a rattlesnake curled up in her front yard. Since it wasn't an emergency, I Googled the local non-emergency line and gave them a ring. They put me through to the fire department, who swooped in and saved the day by getting rid of the sneaky snake!

If you are in the UK, you'll want to learn the different emergency or help numbers available and when to call which one. For help you can check out the article titled Phoning 999, 112, 111 or 101: Which Number is Best? by Cory Jones found on firstaidtraining-cooperative.co.uk.

Tip & Action: *To prepare ahead of time you can take a picture of your applicable chart below and save or favorite it in a way that is easy to recall. You could also save the numbers in your phone as a contact, or write them down and keep it in an easy to access place like your wallet.*

IF YOU OR SOMEONE YOU KNOW IS IN CRISIS OR STRUGGLING, HELP IS AVAILABLE

IN AN EMERGENCY
   Call (or text) 911 or go to the nearest emergency facility
      (emergency facilities: fire station, police station, hospital ER)

IF URGENT
   Call or text 988 or chat on 988lifeline.org
   Text MHA to 741741 to connect with a trained Crisis Counselor

---

Canada & United Kingdom

IF YOU OR SOMEONE YOU KNOW IS IN CRISIS OR STRUGGLING, HELP IS AVAILABLE

IN AN EMERGENCY
   Call 911 (CA) or 999 (UK) -or- go to the nearest emergency facility
      (emergency facilities: fire station, police station, hospital ER)

IF URGENT
   (CA) Call the Crisis Services Canada hotline at 1-833-456-4566
         Text CONNECT to 686868 to connect with a trained Crisis Responder
   (UK) Call Childline 0800 1111 -or- Samaritans 116 123
         Text SHOUT to 85258 to connect with a trained Crisis Counselor

---

If you are in need of support, but not in crisis, consider reaching out to a warmline. Warmlines offer a place to call when you just need to talk to someone. Speaking to someone on these calls is confidential, usually free, and run by people who understand what it's like to struggle with mental health problems.

Tip & Action: *To find a warmline go to (US) mhanational.org/warm lines, (CA) cmha.ca clicking [Find Help], or (UK) mind.org.uk and click the red [Get help now] button.*

COOKING CONFIDENCE

Nutrition & Food

Cooking truly is a gateway to independence and wellness. Starting with a foundation of nutritional awareness, you can craft meals that are both nourishing and enjoyable. Incorporating a variety of ingredients not only enhances flavor but also ensures a well-rounded intake of essential nutrients.

Taking charge of your own cooking means you have control over what goes into your meals, allowing you to make healthier choices and avoid the excess salt, sugar, and unhealthy fats often found in restaurant dishes. Plus, cooking at home is usually more cost-effective, saving you money in the long run.

Exploring different recipes and experimenting with flavors can be a delightful journey of culinary discovery. Whether you're following along with cooking channels or using apps to explore new recipes and ingredients, there's always something new to try in the kitchen.

Tip & Action: *Start by picking two healthy and balanced recipes for each meal. Get comfortable with buying the ingredients and making the meals. Here are some easy ideas to get you started:*

- *Breakfast: Veggie omelet, pancakes/crepes, oatmeal, or a breakfast burrito.*
- *Lunch/Dinner: Spaghetti with ground beef and carrots or meat and white rice with broccoli.*

Start with these recipes, and once you know them well, add more to your list. Happy cooking!

Creating a meal plan and grocery list is a fantastic way to stay organized and ensure you have everything you need for your meals throughout the week. By listing out the ingredients for each meal and considering how many times you'll be making them, you can streamline your grocery shopping process and minimize food waste.

In addition to traditional cooking methods, tools like slow cookers and pressure cookers can be incredibly convenient for busy schedules. With these appliances, you can prepare delicious meals with minimal hands-on time, allowing you to focus on other tasks while your meal cooks to perfection.

Exploring recipes for soups, stews, pasta dishes, and even desserts opens up a world of culinary possibilities with these versatile appliances. Even when you are new to cooking, incorporating these tools into your kitchen can make meal preparation both efficient and enjoyable.

By honing your cooking skills and embracing creativity in the kitchen, you're not only nourishing your body but also feeding your sense of adventure and self-sufficiency. So, roll up your sleeves, grab your apron, and let's get cooking!

***Tip & Action:** If you go to frompenniestoplenty.com you can find "100 Cheap Meals for When You're Broke" and see delicious, healthy, and cheap meals you can whip up.*

Reading ingredients and nutrition labels helps you make healthier choices when shopping for or eating new food. It shows you what you're putting into your body and helps you avoid unhealthy ingredients. Websites like EatRight.org have guides to help you read nutrition labels.

Staying informed about common food myths can prevent you from following fad diets or unhealthy eating habits. NutritionFacts.org uses scientific research to debunk common food myths.

In the "Whole Foods" webpage (NYC Department of Health and Mental Hygiene, n.d.), we learn "whole foods are foods that have not been processed. When food is processed, fat, sugar and salt are usually added and important nutrients, such as fiber, are usually removed. Too much saturated fat, added sugar or sodium can increase your risk of developing a chronic disease.

Whole foods include fresh fruits and vegetables, whole grains (such as oats, brown rice and barley), nuts, beans, fish, shellfish and eggs. Minimally processed foods are foods that are a little processed, such as frozen produce or whole wheat flour. Eating mostly whole or minimally processed foods, when possible, can help you stay healthy."

Nutrition planning can be easier with advice from professionals like healthcare providers or certified nutritionists. They can help you create a plan that works best for you. Your family can also help a lot with this!

Tip & Action: *Talk with your close and extended family too and see what nutrition plans work well for them, and likely you too, considering your similar genetics, heritage, culture, and location.*

For a nutrition plan example, a moderately active 14-18-year-old boy might need 1,800-2,000 calories per day. A balanced diet for him could be 40% carbs, 30% protein, and 30% fat. When you read food labels, look for these percentages to plan your meals better and stay healthy.

Tip & Action: To better understand nutrition labels and know what you are consuming, you can use an app like "Food - Calorie & macro tracker," even if just for a week or two, to become familiar with what you are consuming and what healthy changes you could make, like increasing protein intake.

Nutrition Facts

___servings per container
Serving size ___ cups (___g)

Amount per serving
Calories _____

	% Daily Value*
Total Fat ___ g	%
Saturated Fat	%
Trans Fat	
Cholesterol	%
Sodium	%
Total Carbohydrate	%
Dietary Fiber	%
Total Sugars	
Includes	%
Protein	
Vitamin D	%
Calcium	%
Iron	%
Potassium	%

* The % Daily Value (DV) tells you how much a nutrient in a serving of food contributes to a daily diet. 2,000 calories a day is used for general nutrition advice.

When shopping for food, it's important to know about expiration dates (when the food should be eaten by) and best-by dates (when the food might not taste as fresh). Make sure the expiration date is after you plan to eat the food. For example, don't pick a ketchup bottle that expires in two months if it will take you six months to use it all.

When picking fruits and vegetables, avoid ones that are limp, soggy, moldy, or discolored. You can look up tips online, like "how to pick the best watermelon," to help you choose the freshest produce.

It's also important to store your food properly. Here are some food storage tips:

- Bananas: Separate each banana from the bunch to make them last longer.
- Apples: Keep them in the fridge to stay fresh and crispy.
- Tomatoes: Store them at room temperature, not in the fridge, to keep their flavor.
- Bread: Keep it in a cool, dry place or freeze it to make it last longer.
- Potatoes: Store them in a cool, dark place, like a pantry, but not in the fridge.
- Onions: Keep them in a cool, dry place, away from potatoes, to prevent them from spoiling faster.
- Leafy Greens: Store in the fridge in a plastic bag with a paper towel to absorb moisture.
- Milk: Keep it in the coldest part of the fridge, usually at the back, not in the door.
- Nuts: Store them in an airtight container in the fridge or freezer to keep them fresh.

US Food System Problems & Solutions

When I buy food, I look for items with the least ingredients, like single-ingredient foods. I focus on organic whole foods that are ethically raised, grown, and harvested. I try to make the most of my diet with these foods.

I prioritize organic food to avoid consuming toxins like pesticides and extra hormones. This is especially important in the US. When I buy meat, I usually get organic grass-fed ground beef because it's cheaper and easier to cook. For eggs, I choose organic ones. The labels cage-free, free-range, and pasture-raised tell you about the hens' living conditions. Pasture-raised hens have the most room, sunshine, and nutrients, which means their eggs are healthier.

Tip & Action: *You can learn more about the nuances of eggs and chickens in another one of my books, "Raising Chickens: A Guide to Help You from Hatch to Harvest" by Joy Pack: Stay updated on all my projects; make sure to visit my website, join my email list, or explore my Amazon author page. You can find QR codes and links at the very end of this book for quick reference.*

Apps like "EWG Healthy Living" can help you learn about ingredients and their potential harms in foods and other products like lotion and makeup. For produce, remember the "Dirty Dozen" and "Clean Fifteen." The Dirty Dozen is a list of produce most contaminated with pesticides, so try to buy organic for those. The Clean Fifteen has the lowest pesticide residues, so non-organic is okay.

The current list is found under the EWG's Shopper's Guide to Pesticides in Produce™ (EWG, 2024)...

DIRTY DOZEN: Strawberries, Spinach, Greens (kale, collard & mustard), Grapes, Peaches, Pears, Nectarines, Apples, Peppers (Bell & Hot), Cherries, Blueberries, Green Beans.

CLEAN FIFTEEN: Avocados, Sweet corn, Pineapple, Onions, Papaya, Sweet peas (frozen), Asparagus, Honeydew melon Kiwi, Cabbage, Watermelon, Mushrooms, Mangoes, Sweet Potatoes, Carrots.

Cooking Process & Safety

Before you start your cooking adventure be sure to first wash your hands and put an apron on for protection if desired. Then, remember that safety in the kitchen is super important. Knowing how to use kitchen tools like knives and hot pans can help you avoid accidents. Websites like thekitchn.com have great tips on kitchen safety, including how to use knives properly. So, as you cook, keep your focus on both making delicious food and staying safe.

Cooking new and fun recipes is exciting, but always prioritize safety. Here are some tips:

Knife Safety & Knowledge

- Sharp Knives: Always use a sharp knife. Dull knives can slip and cause accidents.
- Types of Knives:

  - Chef's Knife: The superhero of knives! Great for chopping veggies, slicing meat, and smashing garlic.
  - Paring Knife: Small and perfect for peeling fruits or cutting strawberries.
  - Serrated Knife: Looks like a mini saw. Great for cutting bread or soft fruits without crushing them.

- Using Knives:

  - Use a stable cutting board.
  - Keep your hands dry.
  - Hold the knife firmly with fingers away from the blade.
  - Always cut away from yourself.

- If a knife falls, step back and let it drop. Don't try to catch it!
- Never leave knives in the sink or with the blade facing up.

Stove and Oven Safety

- Stay Focused: Always pay attention to what you're cooking. Avoid distractions.
- Handles and Flammable Items: Turn the pot and pan handles inward. Keep dish towels and paper towels away from burners.
- Fire Safety: Know how to use a fire extinguisher or blanket. If you smell gas or notice something wrong with appliances, turn them off and get help.
- Oven Use:

  - Use oven mitts or potholders for hot dishes.
  - Preheat the oven before cooking and set timers to avoid burning food.
  - Leave the timer going until you take the food out to remember.

Microwave Safety

- No Metal: Never put anything metallic, like aluminum foil or metal utensils, in the microwave. It can cause a fire.

Cleaning Up

- After cooking, turn off all appliances.
- Clean up after yourself by following what you used and did from start to finish. Clean any spills on the stove and

crumbs on the counter, and put everything back where it goes.

Enjoy your delicious meal and the independence of cooking! Remember, safety comes first; then, always keep and leave it clean.

FINANCES

Managing your money is like being the boss of your own wallet! It starts with budgeting, which is like making a game plan for your cash. First, figure out how much money you're bringing in each month. Then, decide where it should go: some for saving, some for spending, and some for emergencies.

You can use tools like Google Sheets to keep track of your spending. It's like having a digital piggy bank that you can access from anywhere. Even big-shots use it to stay on top of their finances!

Budgeting isn't just for grown-ups with big bucks. Even if you're just splurging on a snack or hitting the movies with friends, you can track it. The key is to make sure you're not spending more than you're bringing in.

Let's break it down: say you're a 17-year-old with a part-time gig and some allowance money. You earn $500 a month, plus $100 in allowance. After putting some in savings and covering things like food, transportation, and fun stuff, you're left with $200 to spare.

A good rule to follow is the 50-30-20 plan. That means 50% for things you need, like food and shelter, 30% for wants, like streaming services and fun outings, and 20% for saving up for big goals or emergencies. With a budget like that, you're the boss of your bucks!

Tip & Action: *Write out your budget, even if it's simple. If you have bank accounts, organize them and decide what each account is for. Aim to have over $1,000 in savings!*

Tip & Action: *Visit consumer.gov/managing-your-money/making-budget to get a walkthrough and details on budgeting. Consumer.gov is a service of the Federal Trade Commission (FTC) and provides practical information to help consumers understand their rights and make informed decisions about their finances, credit, loans, and scams. The site offers resources and advice on a wide range of topics, including managing money, dealing with debt, and avoiding fraud.*

Being thrifty is something to feel good about! There are many things that can help you save money and live a more sustainable life. Some tips are to use glass containers for storing food, turn off water, lights, fans, and other appliances when not in use, freeze leftovers, buy misshapen fruit, buy from local food producers, reduce, reuse, recycle. These not only save you money but help protect and care for your community and planet!

A smart thing to do with your budget is to set a spending limit with a waiting period. This helps you avoid impulse buys when there's a sale or a pushy salesperson. Remember, there will always be another sale, so don't rush into buying something that's not right for you. For example, if you have a $200 "sleep on it" rule, any purchase over $199 needs at least 12 hours of thinking time. For bigger buys, decide your max price ahead of time and learn about the product and price before shopping.

Interest, Savings, Debt & Credit

Interest is powerful; it can either work for you or against you. Simple interest is a fixed amount you pay on the original loan amount without adding extra interest over time. Compounding interest is more common with loans. It means you pay interest on both the original amount and the interest that builds up over time, making your total balance grow.

Tip & Action: *To learn more and see how different types of loans can affect you, start with a Google Search for "different types of interest."*

Warren Buffett is one of the best investors in the world and usually one of the top 5 billionaires ($106B in 2023). Buffett says compound interest is an investor's best friend. He compares building wealth through interest to rolling a snowball down a hill: (Gautam, 2023) "I started building this little snowball at the top of a very long hill. The trick to have a very long hill is either starting very young or living to be very old."

The same can be true when compound interest works against you, like with credit card debt or student loans, if you don't pay them off quickly. Albert Einstein said, "Compound interest is the eighth wonder of the world. He who understands it earns it … he who doesn't … pays it." Compound interest can impact your money, but it also affects other things like your knowledge and health decisions.

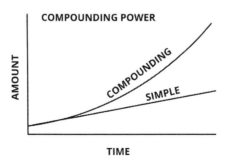

Tip & Action: *An excellent book on exponential compounding about the choices you make in all areas of life is* The Compound Effect *by Darren Hardy (2012).*

Saving and investing can be like planting seeds for a bright financial future! Start by planning your budget to set aside money for savings and emergencies. One cool trick is to set up direct deposit into a separate savings account with a good interest rate. Then, forget about it! Only dip into that account when you hit your goals or have a real emergency. Trust me, the security and peace of mind you get from having savings are worth way more than any impulse buy.

Now, let's talk about emergency cash. It's like your financial safety net! I like to have different bank accounts for different purposes. Start with one for regular expenses, then have two savings accounts: one for short-term goals and one for emergencies and long-term savings. It's all about being prepared for the unexpected.

Ever heard of the cash and envelope budgeting technique? It's super simple and effective! Here's how it works: divide your monthly income into different spending categories like groceries, entertainment, and utilities. Then, get some envelopes and label each one with a category. Put the budgeted cash into each envelope.

Throughout the month, only use the cash from each envelope for its specific purpose. Once an envelope is empty, that's it until next month! This method helps you control your spending, see where your money goes, and avoid overspending. Plus, it encourages good spending habits and helps you stick to your budget. You can even level up by moving your leftover cash into a high-interest savings account at the end of each month. Cool, right?

Tip & Action: *Check out some helpful sites and apps for building and protecting your finances: (US) NerdWallet, FatWallet, The Balance, Swagbucks; (UK) MoneySavingExpert.com, TopCashBack, Quidco, or HotUKDeals.*

Debt and loans can be like double-edged swords – they come with both risks and benefits. If you're not careful or don't fully understand them, you might find yourself in hot financial water. So, it's crucial to tread carefully and make smart decisions.

Getting into debt is kind of like making a deal with a money genie. Sure, you get what you want now, but you're also promising to pay it back later and then more! And let me tell you, breaking promises with money genies is not fun! It's important to fully understand what you're getting into before you sign on the dotted line.

One smart move is to use your credit card wisely. I treat mine like a debit card. I only swipe it for stuff I know I can pay off right away, and I make sure to keep up with it every two weeks. That way, I'm in control of my spending and not letting debt boss me around!

Tip & Action: *Before saddling yourself with any debt, use a Payment/Debt Calculator to see what different payment options will cost you over time, making the minimum and then your planned payments.*

Tip & Action: *It is excellent to make payments every two weeks instead of monthly for most large/long debt and compounding interest loans (like Student Loans or a Mortgage).*

Debt can be like a trusty tool in your financial toolbox, but you've gotta handle it with care. When used wisely, it can help you build assets like a home or rental properties down the line. Then, know insurance is debt's must-have partner; for most cases, banks won't lend you money for things like a new car or house unless you first prove insurance on it.

Now, here's the secret sauce: your credit score. It's like your financial report card, and everyone's checking it – from banks to landlords to insurance companies. To boost your score, stick to spending the money you actually have and pay off your debts right on schedule. Trust me, seeing that score climb is a real confidence booster! And the higher it goes, the sweeter the deals you'll snag on loans and other things like rent and insurance rates.

Tip & Action: *You can use Credit Karma (UK & US+) for specific tips on building credit and service to monitor your credit score and factors. They have an app or go to creditkarma.com. I use the app and check it at least monthly; it gives you a report of your score, what impacts it, and how to improve it.*

Tip & Action: *Do you have a responsible adult in your family with a credit score of over 750 who pays off their credit cards at least every two weeks? If so, ask them if they can add you as an authorized user on their credit card. Some banks have no age limit for this. Once added, sign up for CreditKarma and watch your credit build as they use their card, without you having to spend any of your own money.*

My friend was lucky enough to have a mom that responsibly did this for her and she was able to buy a house at a pretty young age when there was a dip in the market and she qualified because of the credit history her mom built for her.

For now, if you have or are thinking about getting a credit card, consider only going into debt with certain boundaries like getting…

1. Gas, or something else simple you already regularly buy, just for building credit.
2. An education where the total amount of debt is no more than the corresponding jobs entry-level or average annual salaries.

3. A vehicle loan when you would not otherwise have a reliable vehicle, and the payment is less than 15% of your monthly income.

Before acquiring a loan, especially a non-simple interest type loan:

1. Figure out the best way to pay it off.
2. Stick to that plan or pay more than your plan scheduled.
3. Don't just make the minimum payments. Pay between your planned amount or your maximum payment amount available.

Tax Basics

Taxes and insurance might seem boring, but they're super important and play a huge part in your life and future!

In a perfect world, taxes are meant to help the government protect, serve, and support its people. The government's most basic job is to keep us safe from threats. After ensuring safety, there are other things that citizens ask the government to take care of. Throughout history and today, governments get the money to do their jobs through taxes. It's our civic duty to pay taxes to help fund what the government provides for us.

US Taxes

Understanding and filing taxes is a skill that can save you a lot of money! Taxes should be part of the budget you create for your financial success. In the US, the IRS (Internal Revenue Service) handles federal taxes. Different places have different tax rules, like states, provinces, and local governments. It's common to pay local, state, and federal taxes, but some local governments don't tax things like sales or property.

There are different types of taxes:

- Income Tax: You pay a percentage of your paycheck to the government.
- FICA Taxes: Social Security and Medicare taxes are taken from your income to fund these government programs. If you have a W2 income job, your employer pays part of this for you.
- Property Tax: Homeowners pay this tax based on the value of their property to local governments. If you're renting, this tax is often included in your rent.
- Sales Tax: This is an extra cost added to things you buy. To avoid overspending, include sales tax in your budget. For example, if a TV costs $100 and your local sales tax is 8%, you calculate 8% of $100 (which is $8) and add it to the price. So, the total cost at the register is $108.

Different items can have different sales tax rates. In some places, groceries might have a low sales tax rate (0-1.5%), essential items might have a medium rate (5-8%), and luxury items might have a higher rate.

The most common tax forms are for employees, entrepreneurs, and self-employed people:

- W-4 Form: This form lets employees choose how much tax should be "withheld" or taken from their paycheck and sent to the government. You fill it out when you start a job or want to change your withholdings. Your employer uses this form to decide how much tax to take out of your paycheck automatically.

- 10-99 Form: This form is for reporting income, not from an employer, like freelance work or self-employment. It's different from the W-4 because no one is taking taxes out for you, so you need to report it yourself.
- 1040 Form: This form is for your Individual Income Tax Return. It helps you figure out how much total taxable income you have and whether you owe more taxes or get a refund for the year.

You need to file your tax returns with the IRS and local governments by a deadline, usually April 15th. If you need more time, you can ask for an extension until October 15th. You can file taxes on your own, but most people get help from an accountant, a firm like H&R Block, or an online system like TurboTax.

Deductions help lower your taxable income, which can reduce the taxes you owe. Deductions include things like student loan interest, mortgage interest, business expenses, and charitable donations. Credits directly reduce the amount of tax you owe, like the child tax credit. Most people, especially teens, take the standard deduction.

According to the IRS, "For 2023, the standard deduction amount has been increased for all filers. The amounts are as follows: Single or Married filing separately—$13,850. Married filing jointly or Qualifying surviving spouse—$27,700." This means if you're a teen or young adult, you subtract $13,850 from your income, then figure out your tax bracket and pay taxes based on that lower number.

There are many details to review and possibly input into a tax calculation. However, as an example for Federal taxes, if I was 17 again (single and childless) in 2023, my calculation would look something like…

1. I made $24,000.00 from the one part-time job I had that year
2. I take the standard deduction of $13,850.00
3. My income to calculate tax from was $10,150.00 (24000 - 13850)
4. All my income would be in the 10% Tax bracket rate
5. In total, I would owe $1015.00 in Federal taxes for 2023 (10150 x .1)
6. My W2 from 2023 shows I paid $1200.00 in Federal income tax that year
7. In the end, I would get a tax refund from the IRS of $185.00 (1200 - 1015)

If you've paid more taxes than you owe, you'll get a refund. But if you've paid less, you'll have a balance to pay. You can set up payment plans if you need help paying it off. If this happens to me, I'd increase the taxes taken out of my paycheck or save more money for next year. Most people prefer getting a tax refund instead of saving up to pay a balance they owe.

Canada & UK Taxes

The UK and Canada share the same monarchy, and their tax systems share some broad principles. They also have many different rules and structures. Here are some key points to high-light the similarities:

1. Progressive Income Tax: Both countries use a progressive income tax system, meaning higher incomes are taxed at higher rates.
2. Value-Added Tax (VAT) / Goods and Services Tax (GST): Both have a form of consumption tax. The UK has VAT, while Canada has GST and HST (Harmonized Sales Tax) in some provinces.
3. Tax Credits and Deductions: Both countries offer various tax credits and deductions to reduce taxable income.

Healthcare Coverage Basics

In the world of healthcare, having coverage is like having a shield against big medical bills. In the US, you can get health insurance from your job, private companies, or government programs like Medicaid and Medicare. You pay a fee, called a premium, and in return, you're covered for stuff like doctor visits, hospital stays, and even prescriptions. But watch out for those extra costs, like copayments and deductibles.

In places like the UK and Canada, healthcare is more of a community thing. Their systems, like the National Health Service and Medicare, are funded by everyone's taxes. So, when you need medical help, you're covered with no extra bills attached.

__Tip & Action:__ To help find where to purchase prescriptions at the best price, you can compare your insurance price with the app 'GoodRx: Prescription Saver' or the website goodrx.com. They help track prescription drug prices in the US and provide coupons for medication discounts.

Teens should have a yearly check-up with a healthcare provider and regular dentist visits to stay healthy. It's important to have open and honest talks with your doctors about any health concerns. If you need specialized care, see a specialist. Your doctors are there to help you, not judge you. Find providers who make you feel safe, empowered, and respected.

Whether you have your own insurance or are on your parent's plan, you can get copies of your insurance documents. This includes your insurance card, which you should carry with you or have a photo of on your phone. The card has info about your coverage and how to contact your insurance provider. You can also get an explanation of benefits, which shows the costs and coverage details for healthcare services, including what the insurance company will pay and what you will owe.

Home and Auto Insurance

Insurance is like having a shield around your life and an umbrella to stay dry on a rainy day. Home insurance protects you from stuff like fires, storms, and even theft. Plus, it covers your stuff inside and helps out if someone gets hurt on your property. You pay a fee called a premium, and if something bad happens, you pay a bit upfront, called a deductible. Then, your insurance swoops in to save the day!

For auto insurance, it kicks in if your car gets damaged, stolen, or if you accidentally bump into someone else's ride. There are different types, like collision for accidents and comprehensive for other stuff like theft or nature mishaps. Just like home insurance, you pay a premium and a deductible when you need to make a claim.

Remember, your deductible is the money you pay first before your insurance steps in. So, if you scuff your car and it costs $2,000 to fix but your deductible is $500, you'd pay the $500, and your insurance would cover the remaining $1,500.

Tip & Action: *It is a good practice to get your own quotes and price out the repair of your home, belongings, or vehicle before you file a claim. So first, get a quote and ensure the cost is higher than your deductible and the total after the deductible is more than you want to or can reasonably pay. Once you talk to the claims department and file a claim, it usually stays on your record even if they don't pay anything.*

To keep your ride safe-Lock up your car, park in safe spots, and don't leave valuables lying around. And don't forget to give your car some TLC with regular maintenance, and always keep your eyes on the road!

To prevent losses to your home, belongings, and personal liability. Stay on top of home upkeep, lock those doors and windows tight, and stash spare keys in smart spots. Trim your yard, light up your home with security systems and motion-activated lights, and build that friendly rapport with your neighbors for extra security. Mind your manners, keep valuables hidden, have fire extinguishers handy, and plan for emergencies.

Tip & Action: *for a fun resource on manners to secure more respect, safety, and work to avoid things like a legal lawsuit, check out Brooke Romney's "52 Modern Manners for Today's Teens" Boar book on Amazon.*

Tip & Action: *An easy way to inventory your belongings is to clean your room and spaces and put things away. Then, do a video walk-through of each room and show the belongings in the drawers, cupboards, and closets. If there are higher ticket items with serial numbers, catch those in the video or in separate photos. Then, you can email those to yourself or save them to your Google Drive so you can access them even if your house burns down or all your stuff is stolen.*

You can also use apps like Sortly: Inventory Simplified to inventory your belongings.

When you have vehicle insurance, you'll get insurance identification cards, similar to health insurance cards. These cards show contact information for your insurance provider and details about your coverage and deductibles. Keep this card handy in your vehicle. You can usually get the most up-to-date version online or in the company's app.

Another crucial document to review is the Declarations Page. Here, you'll find all the nitty-gritty details about your coverage, deductibles, prices, and any discounts or factors affecting your rates. Taking a close look at this page helps you grasp exactly what your insurance includes. Personally, I like to choose companies with agents you can build a relationship with. They're handy for guiding you through options, offering direct advice when you're making a claim, and even sharing some neighborly tips and tricks!

TECHNICAL SKILLS

Organizing your digital files is super important for staying on top of things and finding what you need when you need it. Make sure to divide your files into folders and group similar stuff together. Give your files clear names so you can easily search for them later. Adding dates or version numbers can also help keep things organized, especially if you're working on lots of drafts. And don't forget to back up your files regularly to avoid losing them if something goes wrong with your device!

Now, let's talk about leveling up your skills for the future. You might already know some techie stuff, but there's always room to learn more. Ever thought about diving into coding? Languages like Python, JavaScript, or HTML could be your jam. Or maybe you're into data tools like Excel or PowerPoint. Even artistic skills like Photoshop or Premiere could be cool to explore. And hey, don't forget about AI – it's the future! Think about what you enjoy and what you want to learn next to take your skills to the next level.

Speaking of AI, it's not just for sci-fi movies anymore. AI tools like ChatGPT can be super helpful for learning and homework. You can ask questions related to your studies or get clarification on tricky topics. Plus, it can help with writing by suggesting ideas and even changing up your writing style. It's like having a super-smart study buddy right at your fingertips!

But remember, while AI is pretty awesome, it's always a good idea to fact-check important info with reliable sources. And hey, did you know you can even use AI to create art? Sites like Midjourney or DALL-E can help you get creative and make some seriously cool stuff. Just give them the right prompts, and they'll do the rest. So go ahead, embrace the power of AI, and let your productivity and imagination run wild!

Now, when you are outside your home, how do you prepare for the moments of physical worry and stress? How can you avoid the feelings and consequences of being unprepared?

CHAPTER TWO
PHYSICAL SKILLS FOR OUTSIDE THE HOME

N ow, here is step 2! Do you know what you would do if you came across an emergency? How would you handle a car malfunction? How can you safely get where you want to go?

FIRST AID

Being first aid savvy is like having a personal med pack you get to whip out when someone's hurt or feeling sick suddenly. Your main missions? Keep them safe, stop any bad stuff from happening, and help them feel better until the pros show up. Knowing even the basics of first aid can be the game-changer in emergencies, and it's a major confidence booster, too!

So, what's in this first aid arsenal? Treating cuts, wounds, burns, and those pesky little injuries that pop up unexpectedly. Want to level up your skills? There are cool apps like "First Aid: American Red Cross" that can teach you all sorts of lifesaving tricks. Plus, the websites for redcross.org & firstaidtrainingcooperative.co.uk are packed with helpful info on handling different emergencies.

And don't forget your trusty first aid kit! Keep one handy at home and pack a mini-version for your adventures outside. Whether you build it yourself or snag a ready-made one, make sure it's easily accessible, fully loaded, and you know what's tucked inside.

Tip & Action: I carry a small first aid kit in my purse on the go that has come in handy many times. It contains a few bandaids, alcohol prep pads, tiny travel spray bottles of rubbing alcohol and hydrogen peroxide, burn cream, and an antibacterial ointment. You could use a little travel bag or just a quart-size ziplock. Now, you can be more prepared everywhere you go!

Medical Emergency Responses

Knowing about common health emergencies can help you react the right way and prevent things from getting worse. In any emergency in the US or CA, you can call the emergency line, 911, for help.

In the UK you should call 999 for emergencies, and if you need non-emergency medical help and advice call 111 for the NHS. The operators are trained to guide you through what to do on the phone until professionals arrive to take over.

Get ready to be a health hero! Knowing these medical issues can help you take better care of yourself and others:

- CARDIAC ARREST: When someone suddenly can't respond, breathe, or has no pulse, call 911 and start CPR. Learn CPR at www.redcross.org/take-a-class/cpr/performing-cpr.
- CHOKING: If someone's having trouble breathing or can't cough, do 5 back blows and 5 abdominal thrusts. Alone? Contact Emergency Services, and don't hang up! For more,

search YouTube for "American RedCross Heimlich how to."

- SEIZURES (INCLUDING EPILEPTIC SEIZURES): If someone is having a seizure, stay calm and clear the area of sharp objects. Cushion their head, turn them onto their side to help with breathing, and time the seizure duration. Do not restrain them or put anything in their mouth. Call emergency services if the seizure lasts longer than five minutes, the person is injured, they have difficulty breathing afterward, or if it's their first seizure. Stay with them until medical help arrives.
- STROKE: Recognize weakness, confusion, or slurred speech? Call 911, note the time, and keep the person calm.
- HEATSTROKE: If someone is overheated, move them to shade, cool them down with water, and fan them. Stay hydrated and take breaks from heat.
- HYPOTHERMIA: If someone is shivering and cold, get them warm, remove wet clothes, and offer warm drinks. Dress in layers and stay dry to prevent it.
- SEVERE ALLERGIC REACTION: Swelling or trouble breathing? Use an epinephrine auto-injector (if available) and call 911.
- MAJOR TRAUMA: Severe injuries? Call 911, provide first aid, and stay with the person until help arrives.
- DIABETIC EMERGENCIES: Confusion or extreme thirst? Give sugar for low blood sugar and encourage taking prescribed insulin for high blood sugar.
- RESPIRATORY DISTRESS/FAILURE: Trouble breathing or wheezing? Call 911 and assist with prescribed inhalers.
- BURNS: Cool the burn with water, apply burn cream, and cover with a bandage.
- FAINTING: Lay the person down, elevate their legs, and call for medical help if needed.

- POISONING: If someone shows symptoms of poisoning, call 911 and remove them from the source if safe. Check for breathing and provide care as needed.

Remember these steps, and you'll be a health hero in no time!

In an emergency, your help can make a big difference. Call for help and stick with the person who needs it. If they're in danger, like on a busy street, move them carefully. Stay calm, watch what's going on, and remember details for the pros.

Take a first aid class at a local center to learn more. Know where the nearest hospital is and keep important numbers handy. Groups like the American Red Cross and Mayo Clinic have lots of health info. And apps like WebMD can give you quick answers when you need them.

Tip & Action: *Find the nearest emergency room to your common locations, like home and school. If you have pets, you can do the same for animal hospitals. Make a quick reference, like saving it on your phone or posting it on your fridge.*

TRANSPORTATION

Mastering public transportation is key in city living or travel. It's eco-friendly and budget-friendly! Get familiar with bus or subway routes and how to read transit maps. Being savvy with public transit is a game-changer for getting around town.

Apps like Google Maps are handy but have a backup plan in case of delays or closures. Stay alert and keep your belongings safe from swipers while commuting. Still, knowing how to read maps is a useful skill, especially when tech fails. It also helps you understand your surroundings better. Check out Map Reading Skills for tutorials.

For short trips, riding a bike or scooter is awesome. It's a fun way to stay active and connect with nature, your body, and your community. Learn how to fix a flat tire or adjust the brakes to avoid trips to the shop. Websites like REI Expert Advice at rei.com/learn/c/cycling have great tips. Always wear a helmet and follow traffic laws to stay safe.

Even if you don't own a car, knowing some car basics can be super helpful. Whether it's your car or someone else's, understanding how it works and how to maintain it is useful. Always check the car's manual for specific instructions.

When you're ready to get your driver's license, take time to practice, be patient, and learn your local driving laws. This is super important for your safety, your car, and everyone around you. Stay calm and patient with those helping you. Remember, all this effort is to give you more freedom and options while keeping you safe!

Tip & Action: *Keep on task once it's over, check out this video of Haley taking her driving test (Modern Family Clips, 2020, Haley takes her driver's test). Here we are reminded why it is so serious to stay aware and drive well!*

When driving, always stay focused, avoid distractions like your phone, and follow traffic rules. Park safely and keep essential supplies in your car for roadside emergencies. Keep your insurance and registration handy in the front of your car. Before you put the car in gear, do everything you need to on your phone—set up your music, start your GPS, or respond to messages—then put your phone down and don't touch it again unless you're completely stopped and in park.

When you operate a vehicle, check for and maintain items like a spare tire, jack, and first aid kit in the trunk or storage area:

- BASIC: warning triangle or cone, jumper cables, a spare tire, tire-changing tools, a first-aid kit, and some water and food.

  In the UK, there is a law that each car must have an emergency reflective triangle and display it 45 meters (about 150 ft) behind your car when you are broken down on the highway. That is a good safety practice to follow anywhere.

- NEXT LEVEL: tire pressure gauge, small containers of motor oil and coolant for topping off fluids if needed, a fire extinguisher, a reflective vest, flares or extra reflective triangles or cones, a flashlight, emergency blanket, duct tape, gloves, tow straps or ropes, chargers, paper map, cash, and emergency contact information. Like a first-aid kit, all these supplies can be purchased in ready-made kits or assembled independently.

Learning how to fix or change a flat tire is super useful and can save you time and money. Flats happen, so being prepared is key. If it's a small puncture, like from a nail, you can patch it up with a tire plug kit and drive to a tire shop or home. This kit usually includes tools to clean the hole and insert a plug. Just follow the instructions and fill the tire with air, if possible, before driving.

If the tire is too damaged, you'll need to replace it with the spare tire. The steps are straightforward, but safety is crucial. Check out tutorials and follow safety guidelines. If unsure, ask for help from roadside service or someone experienced. Practice changing a tire in a safe place with assistance to build confidence.

Steps to Replace a Tire

Materials Needed: Spare (or "donut") tire, jack, lug wrench, vehicle owner's manual, wheel chocks or bricks (optional).

1. Find a Safe Location: Move your vehicle to a flat, stable surface away from traffic. Turn on the hazard lights and engage the parking brake.
2. Locate Spare Tire and Tools: Find your vehicle's spare tire, jack, and lug wrench, usually in the trunk or under the cargo area.
3. Read the Owner's Manual: Check your vehicle owner's manual for specific tire-changing instructions.
4. Use Wheel Chocks (if available): Place wheel chocks or bricks in front of and behind one tire to prevent rolling.
5. Loosen Lug Nuts: Use the lug wrench to slightly loosen the lug nuts on the flat tire while it's still on the ground.
6. Position the Jack: Find the lifting points on the vehicle's frame and place the jack under the car at a designated point.
7. Lift the Vehicle: Use the jack handle to lift the vehicle until the flat tire is off the ground. Ensure stability before proceeding.
8. Remove Lug Nuts and Tire: Fully remove the lug nuts and take off the flat tire. Keep lug nuts in a secure spot.
9. Install the Spare Tire: Put the spare tire on the wheel hub, aligning the holes with the wheel bolts, and push it onto the hub.
10. Hand-Tighten Lug Nuts: Hand-tighten the lug nuts onto the wheel bolts, making sure they're threaded correctly.

11. Lower the Vehicle: Carefully lower the car using the jack until the spare tire barely touches the ground.

12. Tighten Lug Nuts with Wrench: Use the lug wrench to tighten the nuts in a star pattern for even pressure. Tighten as much as possible.

13. Fully Lower the Vehicle: Lower the vehicle entirely using the jack and remove it from under the car.

14. Double-Check Lug Nuts: Ensure lug nuts are secure after fully lowering the vehicle for safety.

15. Secure Tools and Flat Tire: Put all used tools and the flat tire back in your vehicle, ensuring everything is secured.

16. Visit a Professional: Repair or replace the flat tire as soon as possible since spare tires aren't for long-term use.

Another common roadside issue is a dead car, usually because of a dead battery that needs a jump. Always check your car's owner's manual for specific instructions on jump-starting your vehicle or using your tools. One of my favorite Christmas gifts was a portable car jumper from my roommates. I've used it to help myself and others many times. I also keep good jumper cables in my car in case my portable jumper is dead, or the car needing help is too big for it. Watch some tutorials on jumping a dead car and read the following instructions.

Steps to Jump a Car

Materials Needed: Jumper cables, another car with a working battery

1. Safety First: Ensure both cars are parked safely, turn off accessories, and remove keys from ignitions. No open flames are nearby, and metal items are moved away.

2. Position the Vehicles: Park the working car close but not touching the dead one.

3. Identify Battery Terminals: Find the positive (+) and negative (-) terminals. Positive is usually red, and negative typically is black.

4. Connect Jumper Cables:

    A. Attach one red cable end to the dead car's positive terminal.
    B. Connect the other red end to the working car's positive terminal.
    C. Connect one black cable end to the working car's negative terminal.
    D. IMPORTANT: Attach the other black end to an unpainted metal part of the dead car's engine block.

5. Start the Working Car: Let it run a few minutes. Attempt to Start the Dead Car: Try to start the dead car. If no luck, wait a bit and try again.

6. Remove Jumper Cables:

    A. Start with the black cable from the dead car.
    B. Then, the black cable from the working car.
    C. Next, the red cable from the working car.
    D. Finally, the red cable from the dead car.

7. Drive the Jump-Started Car: Drive it for at least 15 minutes to recharge the battery.

Tip & Action: *Look in your owner's manual for specific instructions for jump-starting your particular vehicle. If the car doesn't start after a few attempts or the battery seems damaged, it's advisable to seek professional assistance. If the battery repeatedly goes dead, it may need replacement. Visit a professional for battery testing and replacement if necessary.*

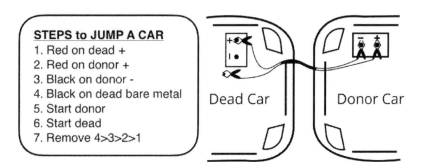

STEPS to JUMP A CAR
1. Red on dead +
2. Red on donor +
3. Black on donor -
4. Black on dead bare metal
5. Start donor
6. Start dead
7. Remove 4>3>2>1

Dead Car   Donor Car

Regular Maintenance

Taking care of your car is important and can be fun, too! Here's how:

Know Your Dashboard: Learn what the warning lights mean, like low gas or engine trouble. Find out where things like the emergency brake and hazard lights are.

Regular Maintenance: Follow the manufacturer's advice for oil changes, coolant, and brake fluid. Check and refill fluids like wiper fluid and power steering fluid. Don't forget to inspect the differential and transfer case fluids for 4WD or AWD cars.

Repairs: A piece-of-mind way to get your car thoroughly checked over is to bring it to a dealership for your manufacturer and have them do a full inspection. I have done this with a handful of my vehicles and have never paid over $150. Then you leave with a full checklist of necessary or fun projects to have them handle or take care of yourself.

Love Your Tires: Keep them inflated, rotate them, and make sure they're aligned. Tire shops usually help inspect and inflate them for free.

Read Your Owner's Manual: It tells you what needs fixing and how often. Be careful with hot parts like the radiator and coolant. YouTube is full of helpful videos for specific cars.

Keep It Clean: Wash your car regularly, tidy up inside, vacuum, and organize your stuff. Have a spot for trash to keep things neat. Taking pride in your car makes driving more enjoyable!

Involvement with the Police & Car Accidents

If you're ever in a car accident, pulled over by the police, or see an accident while driving or riding in a car, there are some good skills to keep you safe and make things go smoothly. You might hear different advice, but I've worked in the insurance industry for many years, have seen and been the victim of a few accidents, and have been pulled over a handful of times.

Getting pulled over by the police can be scary. You might worry about how much a ticket will cost or if the officer will be nice. But I always try to stay prepared, calm, and respectful, assuming that most police officers want to help and keep the community safe.

Know, over 1.3 million people die in car crashes each year worldwide, and many more get injured. There's also a lot of damage to property in each accident. So, police officers are there to help make the roads safer for everyone.

Whenever on a call with Emergency Services, I tell them exactly where I am; I first advise if it is an emergency and medical help is needed or if it is more minor and no emergent medical events are detected. Then I advise them where I am, exactly if possible. Mile markers, street names, and landmarks help. This could sound like, "I am just off the south side of Highway 16 next to mile marker 204."

Tip & Action: *This is where map reading skills, being observant of surroundings, and becoming more directionally aware helps greatly. You can also use apps like Google Maps to pull up the address of a place right next to you or the longitude and latitude of a pin you place at your location.*

In this Google Map mockup, we have an address estimate: [204-296 Morris Presin Dr in Jersey City, NJ]. Then, exact coordinates from Decimal degrees

(DD): [40.6945781, -74.0590150].

If you type those coordinates into the Google Maps search bar, it should bring you to my pin near the Statue of Liberty. You can give an emergency operator the address estimate or the DD coordinates if you have nothing else to go off.

You can also use ///What3Words to provide an exact location via their app or what3words.com. So my pin is at ///jump.jokes.covers

In some cases, the police will not report to an accident scene. Usually, in the US this is because it is on someone else's private property, like a shopping center's parking lot. In the US, the Fourth Amendment to the Constitution of the United States of America. That amendment protects private property against unreasonable searches and seizures by government officials.

If the police are coming, I will wait to exchange insurance information through them. If they do not report to the scene, I exchange information with the other driver. I write down my basic/needed information and exchange it with the driver of the other vehicle. I don't hand strangers my full insurance card or driver's license because those documents have more details on them than a stranger should be privy to, like coverage limits, my home address, or my birthday.

Tip & Action: *The information you want to fully and equally exchange on a separate paper or via texting is: Full name, drivers license number, phone number, insurance company, policy number, and vehicle information (make, model, license plate number, VIN if possible).*

As we discussed earlier when discussing insurance, if my vehicle has damage and I can get quotes from repair shops before speaking with my insurance company, I do so. Then, I evaluate if I want to make a claim. What is the total? What is my deductible? Is the claim on my record worth that price difference?

Here are some tips based on my experience and local laws:

1. Stay Calm and Safe: If you're in an accident, try to stay calm. Make sure your and any passengers are safe. Next, move to the side of the road if you can.
2. Call your Parents and follow their advice. Call 911 (999 in the UK) first if there is a medical emergency.
3. Call for Help: Dial 911 to report the accident and ask for help. Give them your location and any important details, like if there are medical emergencies or if everyone is okay and you just need help sorting it out.
4. Video Recording: (My local laws allow this.) I learned to start a video recording right away after witnessing or being a victim of a few hit and runs. After checking physical safety, I grab my phone and start a video

recording; when I get out of the car, I tuck my phone into the waistband of my pants so it can keep recording as I walk around and talk to the other driver.

5. Exchange Information: If it's safe, exchange information with the other driver. Or I wait for the police.

6. Document Everything: Take pictures (or a walk-around video) of the accident scene, the people and cars involved, and any damage. This will help with insurance claims later.

7. Talk to the Police: When the police arrive, tell them what happened. Be honest and clear, but don't admit fault or place blame; just use true white and black facts for the report.

8. Stay in the Car: If you're pulled over by the police, stay in the car unless they ask you to get out. Keep your hands visible and follow their instructions.

9. See an Accident: If you see an accident involving other cars, don't stop in the middle of the road. If it's safe, pull over and call for help. Don't put yourself in danger.

These tips can help you stay safe and make things easier if you're ever in an accident or pulled over. Remember, it's important to stay calm and follow the instructions of professionals.

QUICK REFERENCE STEPS (copy/save this)

IN A CAR ACCIDENT?

1. **Check for injuries**
   seek medical/emergency help if needed
2. **Reach out to your guardians**
   get their help and follow their guidance
3. **Work with law enforcement**
   if possible and needed
4. **Work through your insurance**
   if a claim is needed on your side

SAFETY & SELF-DEFENSE

The basics of self-defense are super important for your personal safety and confidence. Learning these skills can help protect you and those around you. The main goal of self-defense is to get away from the danger and find help as soon as possible!

The first line of defense is to have situational awareness. Be aware of your surroundings. What kind of place are you in? Who is around? Use this information to scan for safety or possible concerns, and trust your instincts. Just like on airplane safety videos, always identify your nearest exit before proceeding.

When you're out and about, like taking public transportation, it's super important to be aware of your surroundings. Keep your stuff safe by making it harder for anyone to grab your valuables. Use zippers and buttons to secure your things instead of just putting them in open pockets. This way, you're making it tricky for anyone to get to your belongings!

Another thing that can help is your body language. Show confidence and assertiveness by standing tall and making eye contact. Projecting confidence can deter potential attackers. Use a strong and assertive voice when setting boundaries or expressing discomfort. This can attract attention and deter threats.

Good body language and the ability to defend yourself and others improves with better confidence and physical fitness. Role-playing scenarios can help you practice your skills in realistic situations, enhancing muscle memory and decision-making under pressure.

The next level is physical contact self-defense. Use force only when necessary and in proportion to the threat. Remember, there could be legal consequences to self-defense actions, but they are worth the risk if your safety or a loved one's safety is truly on the line. Seek professional training, like a self-defense course or martial arts class, to learn these skills properly.

Tip & Action: *Find a martial art you want to learn and see if there is a local gym in your area that offers a free introductory class. I recently did this with my mother and had so much fun doing it.*

I have wanted to study Krav Maga for many years but recently was inspired by a coworker to take the leap! Krav Maga is a martial art developed for the Israel Defense Forces, and you can study its civilian adaptations. It combines many techniques and is known to focus on real-world applications. I googled Krav Maga and found a few gyms in my area; once I found the one that I wanted to go to (based on location and reviews), then I signed up for a free one-hour intro class. It was a really cool experience, I learned a lot, and it helped me have a better idea of how I can keep learning more.

Learning self-defense can be really useful and boost your confidence! Here are some basics you can start with:

1. Basic Strikes: Learn how to punch, kick, and use your elbows. Focus on vulnerable areas like the eyes, nose, throat, and groin.
2. Basic Blocks: Learn how to protect your face and other soft tissue target areas.
3. Escapes: Techniques like wrist escapes, bear hug escapes, and choke defenses can help you break free from common holds or grabs.
4. Ground Defense: Learn how to escape from beneath an attacker and create space to get up safely.
5. Improvised Tools: Personal items like keys or pens can be used as tools for self-defense if needed.

Remember, the main goal of self-defense is to get away from danger and find help. The best defense is often to avoid dangerous situations whenever you can. Keep talking with trusted friends and adults about personal safety and staying aware of your surroundings.

OUTDOOR SURVIVAL BASICS

Basic outdoor survival skills are valuable for everyone, whether you're a frequent camper, enjoy occasional hikes, or want to be prepared for the unexpected. Learn how to set up a tent, even if it's just a string and tarp from a 72-hour kit or go-bag.

Knowing how to start a fire is essential for warmth, cooking, and signaling for help. Understanding how to read a compass and a map is a lifesaver when technology fails, even in the age of GPS. These skills are helpful for camping and emergencies, like those you prepare for with a go-bag.

Tip & Action: *Build a 72-hour kit or go-bag and take it on a hike or camping trip. Challenge yourself to see how much you can do with just the items in your bag. Practice setting up a tent with a tarp and string from your kit.*

Tip & Action: *In the wilderness, there is a safety tip when dealing with wildlife; the quote goes something like, "In the wild, if it's cute or colorful, leave it alone and don't touch it, because nature didn't care to hide it." You can see this lived out in poison dart frogs.*

If you find yourself in any tough situations, like a medical emergency, car accident, dealing with relational abuse, grief or loss, life changes, or other issues, it's important to be kind to yourself and get the help you need. Many things we go through in life are better handled with good support. Sometimes, talking to a professional counselor can help you process and understand your feelings. Other times, turning to trusted and safe loved ones can provide comfort, guidance, and more safety for you.

Don't hesitate to ask for help!

MAKE A DIFFERENCE WITH YOUR REVIEW

Unlock the Power of Sharing

"Goodness is an investment that never fails"

L.R.

People who share their experiences help others grow and succeed. So if we've got a shot at you doing a ___Tip & Action___ step during our time together, let's do one now!

To make that happen, I have a question for you...

Would you share your thoughts with someone who needs guidance, even if you never met them?

Who is this person that needs guidance? Well, it is someone just like you, and like you used to be before you unlocked some information and skills from this book! We all need direction and support in life.

Our mission is to make Life Skills for Teens Unlocked accessible to everyone. And, the only way for us to accomplish that mission is by reaching...well...everyone.

This is where you come in. Most people do, in fact, judge a book by its cover (and its reviews). So here's my ask on behalf of a struggling teen you've never met:

Please help them by leaving a review for this book

Your gift costs no money and less than 60 seconds to make real, but can change a fellow teen's life forever. Your review could help...

...one more student navigate school with confidence.

...one more teenager plan for their future.

...one more kid succeed in the real world.

...one more parent guide their child through challenges.

...one more dream come true!

To get those 'feel good vibes' and help some people for real, all you have to do is...and it takes less than 60 seconds...**leave a review.**
Simply scan the QR code below,
then leave a review!

If codes or links aren't working for you: just go to Amazon (or wherever you bought this book) and leave a review for the book from there.

Having a hard time thinking what to type?

Just think what you could share that may help a fellow human...

Headline: I loved learning about [favorite topic] from this book!

Review: Share a quick thought about that favorite topic, what you learned, and how you think it will help boost your life.

* Bonus Level * attach a photo to your review! Maybe your favorite page so far, or a screenshot of the **_Tip & Action_** you want to try next…

If you feel good about helping those faceless teens, you are 'my people'. That kind of attitude, energy and action will come back to bless your life immensely!

Now I'm that much more excited to help you master your independence! You'll love the steps and tips I'm about to share in the coming chapters.

Thank you from the bottom of my heart, for your help in guiding success for others! Now, onto your next steps.

One of your biggest cheerleaders, Joy Pack

INTERMISSION

You made it this far!! Congrats! We've covered basic practical and physical skills. Keep learning and developing those. Mastering these skills will boost your confidence, independence, and ability to help others. But don't stop there! To reach your full potential, you need to explore even more.

__Tip & Action:__ Take a little break if needed to open a new page in your notebook, take a moment to leave a review on the book from what you've learned so far, get a refresh, and do whatever else you need to do in this little figurative intermission.

Dive Into Self-Discovery

Now, it's time to roll up your sleeves and get into the nitty-gritty! Let's dig into what makes you, well, you! Understanding yourself on a deeper level builds a strong foundation for growth. We'll explore this together as you work through the book.

As you continue to read, the design of the book is to help you dig deeper into understanding yourself and as you move forward you will likely have a feeling of growing up and maturing alongside the content!

This book is packed with great research and my personal experiences. Try out the tips and see what works best for you. Everyone is different, so find your own style and use the advice here to make your life incredible!

Here's the deal: try things out, see what brings you joy, and keep what works while leaving behind what doesn't. If something seems helpful, double-check it, talk to a pro if needed, and give it a go. Experiment and see what fits you best. These topics will kickstart your journey, give you the basics, and inspire you to explore more about what interests you.

Different Perspectives

Everyone sees the world through their own special glasses, shaped by their experiences and biases. No book can be perfect for everyone, but I hope you find useful stuff here to help you level up in life. In this book, I'll share my tips and experiences. As you grow, you'll develop your own unique way of seeing and interacting with the world.

Learning from the Past

A big key to growth is learning from your past. From fun, silly moments to those that felt like the end of the world but weren't, every experience teaches you something. With a joyful attitude and a commitment to always improve, face life's challenges with an open heart, a smile, and excitement for new experiences.

Unlocking Opportunities

Think of life as a set of doors. Some doors are locked because you're not old enough yet, but some just need the right keys. Those keys are found by learning and applying good information and skills. Many doors get locked behind you on your journey as you age, so be sure to take advantage of your youth while you have it! We'll work together to unlock essential steps, fun life hacks, and supportive tips to help you succeed in your journey through adolescence. Each chapter is a giant step toward mastering your independence.

CHAPTER THREE
DISCOVERING YOUR DEVELOPMENT AND HEALTH

W ant to know something wild? We touched on this a bit in the intro, but adolescence can last into your late 20s!

You might legally become an adult around age 18 but are not developmentally an adult until much later. Understanding and taking advantage of this time of growth is a huge opportunity! Let's look at your development stages, how to take advantage of your growing brain, and how to support your body's development.

YOUR DEVELOPING BRAIN

Puberty and the changes in your body are like a small town transforming into a big city with skyscrapers popping up everywhere. It's a wild and exciting time when everything seems to be under construction!

Childhood ends, and adolescence begins with puberty. It's like the groundbreaking ceremony for all the big changes happening in your body. Puberty usually starts between ages 10 and 14, with some starting earlier and others later. Girls often start and finish puberty earlier than boys. Your brain and body keep developing until about 25 years old, so think of adolescence as a decade-long construction project!

During your teen years, you might feel like parts of your brain are offline, and some familiar paths are now under construction. Puberty can feel scary, confusing, and over-whelming, but it can also be wonderful, exciting, and full of potential for growth and learning.

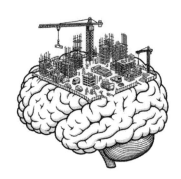

Your "groundbreaking ceremony" has probably already happened, with some plans for your development set by your DNA and genetics. But your choices still matter a lot. What you learn and what you put into your body can significantly impact your development. Think of it as providing better building materials for your construction project, leading to an even more amazing final product.

So, let's talk about the construction process—what changes the most and how long it takes. Then, we'll discuss how to build your most beautiful, strong, and diverse mind ("city").

__Tip & Action:__ To have a solid start to understanding your brain development, watch this TED Talk, "The mysterious workings of the adolescent brain," from neuroscientist Sarah-Jayne Blakemore (June 2012). Pay attention to points that stick out to you. Listen for the limitations and advantages you have at this point in your brain development.

Your brain and body undergo significant changes as you transition from childhood to adulthood. While the limbic region, responsible for emotions and instincts, develops early, the prefrontal cortex, involved in decision-making and self-control, matures later. This delayed development of the prefrontal cortex can lead to impulsive decisions during adolescence. Recognizing these changes can help you navigate this period with patience and make informed choices.

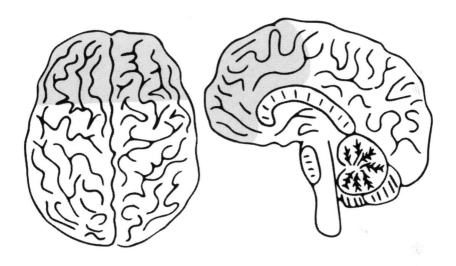

Frontal Lobe

Ever wonder what sets us humans apart from other animals? It's our prefrontal cortex! This part of our brain is like HQ. It's the part of our brain that lets us think ahead, plan, and make decisions about our future. This area is where we design, organize, start new tasks, and adapt to changes. It helps us manage our social behavior, emotions, and personality, and understand social cues to make appropriate social judgments.

Think of it as the bustling heart of the city, where all the action happens. It's where we organize our thoughts, kickstart new projects, and handle social stuff. This part of the brain is also crucial for developing your personality, morals, and impulse control, and we will discuss ways to help promote and balance its best development!

Feeling Misunderstood?

Feeling misunderstood? You're not alone! Sometimes, it seems like no one understands, from our adults to our friends or even in ourselves. But here's the deal: thanks to those helpful hormones, your brain and body are going through a major makeover.

Imagine watching a baby learning to walk. It's thrilling, sure, but also sometimes slow, scary, and frustrating. That's a bit like being a teen. Your brain's prefrontal cortex is busy with construction projects that'll take years to finish. And even though you may look grown-up, your brain is still figuring things out.

So, when adults seem clueless about what you're going through, cut them some slack. Some adults have lost touch with the realities of teen lives and the development they have to go through. However, most adults' brains are just done with major construction, and yours is still a work in progress. It's tough to see things from their perspective, but hang in there. You'll get it.

Do you ever feel judged for your seemingly normal behaviors? Take a step back and ask yourself: am I being safe and respectful? If you are, maybe it's time to try a different approach or just shrug it off and let it roll off your back. You deserve kindness, love, and respect just like everyone else, no matter their age. And remember, most of those "teen troubles" are just part of growing up.

It's all part of the ride, even when it feels like a roller coaster. Just know you're not alone in feeling a bit lost sometimes. This journey is full of ups, downs, and lots of surprises. So, buckle up and enjoy the ride!

YOUR BODY DEVELOPMENT

Your genetics play a big role in some physical changes, but a lot is up to you! Eating well, staying positive, and making good choices give your body the best tools for building a strong, healthy future. Everything you do affects how your body grows and develops, from the food you eat to the thoughts you think. So, make those choices count!

Tip & Action: *Think about or list out what physical changes you have experienced in the last 12 months. How are you different from 1 year ago?*

Puberty means big changes, especially in your reproductive organs and systems. It might feel awkward to talk about, but it's all part of growing up. Knowing what's normal helps you feel more confident.

During puberty, you might feel all sorts of emotions—nervous, excited, self-conscious, and more. It can be overwhelming, but understanding what's happening can make it easier to handle. Talking to trusted adults, like parents or healthcare providers, can help answer your questions and make you feel better about these changes.

Reproductive health and puberty

Before we dive into the next section, let's pause for a moment. If you're a minor, it's essential to have open conversations about reproductive health and healthy sexuality with your parents, guardians, or other trusted adults first. Take some time to chat with them about it. You can even have them read this next part with you and share their experiences with puberty, their perspectives, boundaries, and the importance of healthy sexuality.

Okay, now onto more details and knowledge about reproductive puberty.

Understanding that puberty is a natural and unique process can give you the confidence to navigate this transformative time.

Hormonal changes kickstart puberty in both boys and girls. These changes can cause mood swings, heightened emotional sensitivity, and shifts in behavior. You'll start noticing more body hair, especially in areas like the armpits, pubic region, and legs. Your skin will also undergo changes, like increased oil production leading to acne and shifts in texture. As you grow older, your physical growth will stabilize but continue until you reach your full height. Puberty is considered complete when you've achieved both physical and sexual maturity.

Tip & Action: *For more details on your body, developments, and stages, you can go to kidshealth.org/en/teens/your-body/ & kidshealth.org/en/teens/sexual-health/ and to get a visual of the parts and anatomy on kidshealth.org you can search "Reproductive System" and look at the (for Parents) articles "Female Reproductive System" & "Male Reproductive System."*

Hormones

Both men and women have a set of basic hormones, but their levels and impacts can differ significantly. These hormones include Estrogen, Testosterone, Progesterone, Follicle-Stimulating Hormone (FSH), Luteinizing Hormone (LH), Prolactin, and Oxytocin.

In women, estrogen and progesterone play a key role in regulating reproductive functions and menstrual cycles. On the other hand, testosterone is the primary hormone in men, influencing their physical characteristics and reproductive health. Understanding these hormonal variations helps us grasp the physical and emotional changes that occur during puberty and beyond.

Males

Male puberty brings significant changes to both external and internal reproductive organs. Externally, you'll notice alterations in the penis and scrotum, which houses the testicles. Internally, key organs include the epididymis, seminal vesicle, and ejaculatory duct, crucial for sperm and semen production.

Puberty typically kicks in for boys between ages 9 and 14, bringing several changes:

- Hormonal Shifts and Growth: Testes enlarge, testosterone production increases, triggering growth spurts, muscle gain, and broader shoulders.
- Genital Development: Penis and testes grow, pubic hair appears, and testes begin producing sperm, marking the start of fertility.
- Voice Changes: Larynx grows, deepening the voice with occasional voice cracking. Adam's apple becomes more prominent.
- Facial Hair: Facial hair starts growing, often beginning with a few hairs on the upper lip and spreading gradually.

As puberty progresses, sexual organs mature, and erections become achievable and sustainable. Wet dreams may occur during body adjustments and experiences. While morning erections are common, prolonged or painful erections warrant medical attention.

Understanding these changes helps navigate this exciting but sometimes bewildering time. Remember, everyone develops at their own pace, so if you have concerns, talk to a trusted adult or healthcare provider.

Now, let's discuss some specific hygiene tips for guys. When it comes to aiming when you pee. If aiming is a challenge, consider sitting down to avoid mess. When standing, focus on the task, aim for the bowl, and promptly clean up any drips or spills to keep things tidy.

Fun Fact: The world's longest recorded pee time was almost 9 minutes!

So even if you have record-breaking pee times, it's no more than 10 minutes; just focus on the task, aim for the bowl, and clean up any drips or spills.

Another common issue is inadequate butt hygiene, leading to those "skidmarks" and other unpleasantries. Ensure thorough wiping until the toilet paper comes out clean, and consider using baby wipes or a bidet for a better clean.

Keeping clean is essential and makes a significant difference!

Tip & Action: *For more boy-specific info & tips: Stay updated on all my projects; make sure to visit my website, join my email list, or explore my Amazon author page. You can find QR codes and links at the very end of this book for quick reference.*

Females

Female puberty involves significant changes to both external and internal reproductive organs.

The external genitalia, collectively known as the vulva, include:

- Mons Pubis: The fatty area over the pubic bone.

- Labia Majora: The outer lips.
- Labia Minora: The inner lips.
- Clitoris: A sensitive organ important for sexual pleasure.
- Vestibule: The area surrounding the vaginal and urethral openings.
- Urethra: The tube through which urine exits the body.
- Vaginal Opening: The entrance to the vagina.
- Hymen: A thin membrane that may partially cover the vaginal opening.

The internal organs include:

- Vagina: The birth canal connecting the cervix to the outside of the body.
- Uterus: Where a fertilized egg develops into a fetus.
- Fallopian Tubes: Tubes through which eggs travel from the ovaries to the uterus.
- Ovaries: Organs that produce eggs and hormones.

Females typically begin puberty between ages 8 and 13. Here's what happens:

- Growth Spurts and Body Changes: Girls experience rapid growth, and their hips widen. There's also an increase in healthy body fat around the hips and butt, and the breasts start to develop.
- Genital Development: The vulva grows, and pubic hair begins to appear.
- Menstrual Cycle: The onset of menstrual cycles marks the beginning of fertility. Understanding the hormonal roller coaster of the menstrual cycle can help explain the emotional and physical changes that occur each month.

Understanding these changes can help you navigate puberty with confidence. Everyone develops at their own pace, so it's okay if your experience is different from your friends'. If you have any concerns, talking to a trusted adult or healthcare provider can provide support and guidance.

Menstruation

Male hormone levels tend to have small fluctuations throughout the day, maintaining a relatively stable pattern. In contrast, female hormone levels fluctuate significantly over a month, resembling a roller coaster. This difference explains why menstrual cycles can feel so varied and intense.

Look at its beautiful and complex pattern!

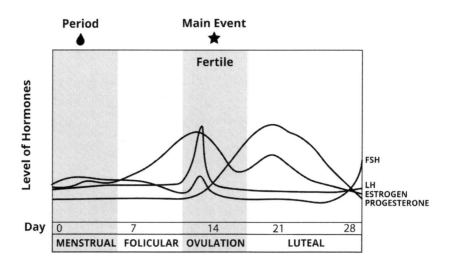

The purpose of the menstrual cycle is to prepare the female's body for pregnancy. Menstrual cycles can vary in length and intensity throughout your life and from girl to girl. A typical cycle lasts about 28 days, so it's usually called a month.

Tip & Action: You can Google *"female hormone cycle chart"* to get more detailed views.

The menstrual cycle begins with the follicular phase, which includes the period or menstrual phase. During this time, the uterus sheds its lining from the previous cycle because there was no fertilized egg to implant. This shedding results in menstrual bleeding. Additionally, in this phase, the ovaries select the healthiest egg to mature and prepare for the next stage.

Girls may experience various symptoms during their period, such as headaches, tiredness, lower back pain, cramps, loose stool, breast tenderness, bloating, or mood swings. The intensity of menstrual cramps can vary depending on factors like the day of the cycle, age, overall health, and potential underlying issues.

When I was younger and first having my periods, around ages 12 to 14, my period cramps were terrible and pretty debilitating for the first day. A lot of times, I would leave school and then just try to sleep it off. As I have gotten older, they have become less painful and troublesome.

My go-to period products and support items are:

- A pair of non-toxic period panties. I wear these at night 1-2 days before my period is coming so that I don't have to worry about leakage if my period starts in the middle of the night.
- A silicone menstrual cup, organic cotton pantiliner, pads, and tampons. I use the cup because of its large capacity and couple it with a pantiliner. I use a pad when I don't want to deal with the cup. I also will occasionally use 100% organic cotton tampons. Sometimes I find my cramps are better if I don't have anything in my vagina.

- Heating pads for my back, stretching, meditation, and anything else that helps me relax like lavender, naps, and warm tea.
- Loose clothing and whatever else makes me more comfortable.
- I focus on hydration and nutrition. Extra water, herbal tea, bananas, milk, and such.
- I take a homeopathic pain reliever if desired like Boiron's Arnica Montana or Earthley's Pain Potion.

Things I avoid when it comes to my period:

- Mainstream/popular tampons, pads, and undies with toxins (carcinogens and endocrine disruptors).
- I try to limit using tampons altogether because of their makeup/ingredients and becoming educated about how they will sluff material off that remains in the vagina, causing imbalances and infections.
- I try to avoid over-the-counter painkillers like ibuprofen and acetaminophen (Tylenol) in general. This is due to the ingredients and health risks. I will, in rare cases, take a small amount of ibuprofen if the pain is more severe.

Ovulation is the star of the show in your menstrual cycle! Imagine you're on a thrilling roller coaster ride at night. As you reach the peak, a dazzling fireworks display lights up the sky above. This is ovulation, where an ovary releases a mature egg that travels down the fallopian tube to the uterus.

Ovulation is a brief yet crucial window for pregnancy, lasting about 24 hours. The fertile period extends a few days before and after ovulation. Signs of ovulation include a slight rise in body temperature and thicker vaginal discharge resembling egg whites.

Following ovulation is the luteal phase, where the body readies itself to shed the uterine lining if pregnancy doesn't occur. This phase may bring on PMS (premenstrual syndrome) symptoms like bloating, mood swings, headaches, water retention, cravings, and breast tenderness. It's all part of the body's natural rhythm, preparing for the next cycle.

Tracking my cycle has been a game-changer for understanding my moods and energy levels. During my fertile ovulation days, I have more energy and feel like I'm in overdrive. But, just before my period starts, I often feel tired, grumpy, or sad. It's like a meme I saw: "When I start my period, and realize that's why I cried over a jelly bean yesterday!" It sounds funny, but it's pretty accurate. Checking my cycle app helps me feel more in control and understand why I'm feeling a certain way.

Understanding and tracking your cycle, or a loved one's, can unveil behavior patterns, aid in planning activities, and foster empathy and awareness. Reproductive health is essential for everyone, regardless of gender. So, take the time to learn about staying healthy and informed!

__Tip & Action:__ You can track menstrual cycles manually or on an app. There are many options, MagicGirl is specifically designed for teens. Natural Cycles: Birth Control is an FDA Cleared Contraception and approved app to track, you use the app coupled with a device, like their thermometer, every morning to get highly accurate information!

Tracking cycles can help you make sense of the monthly scenario many women go through!! The link here is to a TikTok skit about the PMS many women face (disclosure: it has 1 mild curse word in it). And, don't get stuck scrolling!

Menopause might seem far off, but it's a natural part of a woman's life journey. Understanding it now helps you connect better with older women and prepares you for your future. Like puberty, menopause involves significant hormonal changes. Once menopause occurs, women can no longer conceive because their fertility ends. It's all part of the fascinating hormone journey in females.

NEEDS, HEALTH & CARE

There is a cool theory of psychology called Maslow's Hierarchy of Needs that teaches five groups of needs we humans have. It is depicted as levels in a pyramid, from the bottom being foundational physical needs (air, water, food, shelter) to safety (security and resources), belonging (relationships and connection), esteem (respect, self-esteem, freedom) and self-actualization (becoming your best self). By understanding these needs, we can better organize our lives to make sure we feel safe, happy, and fulfilled.

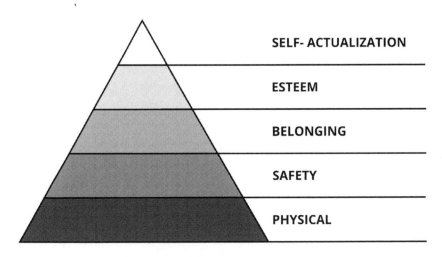

Taking care of our bodies starts with meeting our basic physical needs. That means putting good and healthy things into our bodies while avoiding harmful toxins. Toxins are harmful substances found in various sources like food, water, air pollution, clothing, and even our living environments. While it may seem overwhelming, you can start small by learning about where toxins come from and how to avoid them.

Start by focusing on the basics: breathing purified air, drinking clean water, eating healthy foods, and keeping your living space tidy. Taking these steps one at a time can help you avoid toxins and keep your body healthy as you continue to grow.

Tip & Action: A simple app you can use to check for ingredient health and avoid toxins in your food and products is the EWG Healthy Living app.

Air: Our needs follow a hierarchy based on how long we can survive without them: air, water, food, and shelter. Clean air is our body's primary need. To keep the air around you healthy, avoid things like synthetic chemical scents and mold. Then, consider using an air filter to remove pollutants and dust indoors. Spending time outdoors, especially in areas with less pollution, is also beneficial for your overall well-being.

Water: Next is water. Staying hydrated is crucial for your health. Pay attention to your body's signals—if you're thirsty, you need fluids! A good rule of thumb is to drink about one ounce of water for every two pounds of body weight. However, this can vary depending on factors like age, sex, weight, activity level, health, and climate. In addition to water, you can hydrate with drinks like sports drinks, coconut water, herbal tea, infused water, water-rich fruits, electrolyte drinks, and milk.

A great hack to try if you get headaches (commonly a result of dehydration or low mineral levels) is to take a pinch of cream of tartar (also known as potassium bitartrate) and put it under your tongue until it dissolves. Then, follow it up with a hydrating drink and some light neck and back stretches.

Tip & Action: Find some good recipes to change it up and help you have better hydration. Currently, my favorite tea to drink is a loose-leaf of organic Tulsi Licorice Root.

A yummy recipe for a homemade electrolyte drink (makes one gallon) is: 15 Cups of Water, 1 Cup of Lemon Juice, 3 Tablespoons of Honey, and 1 teaspoon of Mineral-rich Salt.

<u>Tip & Action:</u> A popular book, Your Body's Many Cries for Water by F. Batmanghelidj, M.D. is currently free on Amazon's Audible app and reviews the necessity of hydration and how it can impact health.

Food: Alright, let's talk about food power! It's like the fuel for our bodies, giving us the energy and nutrients we need to rock each day. Think of it as a united team with proteins, minerals, vitamins, fat, fiber, and carbohydrates all playing their part. We get these goodies from lots of yummy sources like meat, eggs, dairy, fruits, veggies, whole grains, and plants. Keeping it simple and fresh is my jam – like steamed broccoli and carrots, juicy ground beef with a sprinkle of salt and pepper, fluffy white rice with a dollop of butter, and a cool hydrating drink. Easy and tasty!

Finding the right food balance is key. Our bodies sometimes need different stuff depending on what's going on – like stress, hormone cycles, or when we're rocking intense activities. It's helpful to team up with pros like healthcare champs or certified nutrition experts to help guide you through your food journey.

<u>Tip & Action:</u> The USDA's MyPlate is a great visual guide for meal planning. You can check it out at myplate.gov. It suggests dividing your plate into sections of roughly 25% vegetables, 25% grains, 20% fruits, 20% protein, and 10% dairy. This can vary based on your needs and goals.

Apps like Food - Calorie & Macro Tracker can help you customize your nutrition plan, especially if you need more protein or other specific nutrients.

Physical Mobility

Make sure to manage stress and prioritize sleep! We'll dig deeper into these skills later, but remember, getting enough shut-eye - around 8 to 10 hours a night - is super important for feeling your best. It might take some trial and error, but trust me, it's totally worth it!

Being active and flexible is also key. Exercise is a big part of that, but it's not just about hitting the gym. Dancing, biking, or even walking your dog all count! And it's not just about getting buff or lean; it's about keeping your heart strong and your body moving smoothly. Plus, mobility - that's all about your joints and how freely you can move. Working on mobility helps you steer clear of injuries and feel fantastic.

So think of "working out" like a three-part plan: strength, cardio (or endurance), and mobility. Together, they're like the ultra trifecta, making you stronger, giving you more energy, and helping you feel awesome!

Tip & Action: *Extremely inspiring and helpful content I have used on mobility training can be found through Amir/Beard, a certified mobility specialist, at BeardTheBestYouCanBe.com or on his Instagram @beardthebestyoucanbe. He has fantastic free content and instructional videos to help with understanding and getting started on a serious mobility journey.*

Having good posture, ergonomics, and alignment is like setting up a strong foundation for your body. Picture your spine as a busy highway for your nervous system, directing all your body's actions.

When your posture or spinal alignment isn't right, it's like having a traffic jam on that highway. Things don't move smoothly, and it can cause issues. But when your skeletal structure is healthy and aligned, it's like clearing out that traffic jam. Your nervous system's connections can flow smoothly, keeping your body working well.

Improper posture and movement can be caused by lots of things, but if you are able to aid or fix them, it can make a big difference in your health and confidence. Some common reasons for misalignment are weak foot and leg muscles, a misalignment in your pelvis or lower spine bones, or tight muscles or ligaments pulling part of your skeleton out of alignment. Often, habits like slouching while using media devices can also contribute. But no matter the cause, working to correct misalignment can improve your health. Standing tall can boost your confidence and make you feel healthier overall.

Tip & Action: *I've found it really helpful to prioritize seeing healthcare professionals who take a root cause approach. Instead of just treating the symptoms, they focus on figuring out what's causing the issue and how to fix it for good. This approach digs deeper to find the real problem and helps you address it from the source.*

I've personally found a lot of relief from physical pain by seeing Chiropractors trained in the Gonstead method. This approach is all about the nervous system and uses detailed analysis and gentle adjustments to realign and balance your body's structure.

Using proper posture and ergonomics is crucial when resting, sitting, moving, exercising, or lifting to prevent misalignment, deterioration, or injury. Ergonomics is a big deal in Corporate America because if you don't use proper posture while working, it can lead to injuries from repetitive movements or improper positions over time. This could result in problems like hernias, slipped discs, headaches, or carpal tunnel syndrome. But you can prevent a lot of pain and injury by maintaining proper posture and movement.

Tip _&_ Action: *To learn more about proper ergonomics, posture, and lifting techniques, do a Google image search for "ergonomic diagrams," "proper lifting techniques," and "proper posture."*

Skin & Hair

Teens often deal with acne, which can pop up because of things like what you eat, how stressed you are, hormone swings, dirt on your skin, or stuff that irritates it. To keep your skin looking good, start from the inside out. Your skin is super important—it's the biggest organ you've got, and it's your first line of defense, so it needs some TLC! Here are some tips to improve your skin health:

1. Healthy Diet: Eat a balanced diet with plenty of fruits, vegetables, and whole foods.
2. Silk Pillowcase: Silk pillowcases are gentle on your skin and can help reduce irritation.
3. Cleanliness: Change and wash your clothes and sheets regularly to avoid dirt and oil buildup.
4. Gentle Exfoliation: Exfoliate your skin gently to remove dead skin cells without causing irritation.
5. Avoid Touching Your Face: Try not to rest your hands on your face to prevent transferring dirt and oils.
6. Sweating and Skincare: Get some exercise to sweat out toxins, then follow up with a good skincare routine.

A solid skincare routine means being gentle with your skin, giving it a little massage, and keeping it hydrated with products that match what your skin likes. If you need extra help, you can try out creams you can buy without a prescription or chat with a dermatologist for pro advice and maybe some medicine.

When you're testing out new skincare stuff or even food or vitamins, start small to see how your skin reacts. For skincare products, dab a bit on the inside of your arm and wait a day to make sure it doesn't cause any trouble. Always follow what the label says and talk to your folks and doc if you're worried or if something doesn't feel right.

Tip & Action: *Simple and small is the best place to start with many aspects of change to your life. With skincare, this can be something like Zendaya's reported 3-step skincare routine. This begins with a simple facial cleanser of African Black Soap, followed by a gentle toner like Rose Petal Witch Hazel, and then moisturize with some Vitamin E Oil.*

Hair problems are a common thing, just like skin issues, and they are directly connected. You might face things like frizz, split ends, greasiness, dandruff, or an itchy scalp. But don't worry; there are simple ways to tackle these troubles at their root, literally, and give your hair some extra love.

One cool trick is using rosemary for your scalp and hair. You can make rosemary water or use rosemary oil. Some other good ingredients are peppermint, ginger, and tea tree (helps to reduce dandruff).

Making rosemary water is easy-peasy: just boil some fresh rosemary in water for about 15 minutes, let it cool, strain it, and then spray it onto your scalp and hair before washing. Or, for the oil mix, add a few drops of rosemary oil with a carrier oil like castor oil and massage it into your scalp once a week. I add a few drops of tea tree in the oil mix, too, if I find I have some dandruff. Then, I make sure to do good scrubbing and exfoliation on my scalp in the shower. These little rituals can help your hair grow stronger and look healthier, plus they smell awesome!

When it comes to styling your hair, it's always fun to get inspiration from social media. Look for influencers who have hair like yours and try out their styles and tricks. This goes for clothing styles, too; I follow people whose style I like and who have a similar coloring and body shape to mine. Then I saw what color pallets, textures, and styles they looked great in. This helps me find things to try that end up looking good on me too. It's a cool way to experiment and find what works best for you!

Sleep

With all the changes happening in your life, your sleep schedule might start to feel a bit off. It's totally normal to find yourself staying up late and wanting to sleep in. This shift happens because your body's internal clock, called the "biological clock," is changing. But it's important to know that your sleep habits can affect your mood, school performance, and health.

Research from the NIH tells us that many teens struggle with sleep deprivation (NIH, National Library of Medicine, 2010). Even though you might want to stay up late, you still have to wake up early for school and other stuff. Your teenage brain needs about 8-12 hours of sleep each night, so try to make a schedule that works for you. Getting enough sleep is super important for your body to grow, heal, and stay healthy. So, don't forget to give yourself some "beauty rest"!

Tip & Action: If your sleep patterns are not providing your mind and body enough rest and recovery, you should work to develop a good sleep schedule. Try to be ready and have your head on your pillow and in bed at least 9 hrs before waking up.

Imagine your body's sleep system as a balanced orchestra, and guess who's the conductor? It's your internal clock, called the circadian rhythm! This rhythm keeps everything in sync, like when to feel awake and when to feel sleepy, all in a neat 24-hour cycle.

Back in ancient times, people woke up with the rising sun and chilled out when it got dark. No bright screens back then, just the gentle glow of stars or cozy firelight. Working with your body's natural rhythm is like tuning into the perfect bedtime symphony. But, uh-oh, sometimes we mess up our rhythm orchestra. Here's how you can help that:

- Say, see ya later to caffeine at least 6 hours before bed. It helps your body not to have to hit the brakes so hard or get stuck with the accelerator.
- Don't munch on snacks or gulp down drinks right before sleeping. Let your stomach chill out for an hour or more before bed.
- Dim the lights to warm, cozy tones like orange or red as bedtime approaches. It's like sending a signal to your body that it's time to wind down.
- Ditch screens for a whole hour before bed! I know it sounds crazy, but trust me, it works. No more scrolling through TikTok or texting pals right before you hit the hay.

And hey, don't panic about the screen time sacrifice. There are tons of cool things to do instead:

- Read a good old-fashioned book.
- Chat with your family or friends face-to-face.
- Stretch out, or meditate for some chill vibes.
- Take a warm bath or practice good ol' hygiene routines.
- Maybe even scribble in a journal or take a leisurely stroll after dinner.

Oh, and here's a pro tip: minimize the energy flowing around you while you snooze. Pop your phone on airplane mode, turn off the Wi-Fi, and set the mood with cozy, dim lighting. Geek out on the details—it can be surprisingly fun and helps you sleep like a champ!

__Tip & Action:__ Setting up that warm screen light feature on your phone is a breeze! Just hop over to YouTube and search for "Night Shift lighting setup on my iPhone" (or your phone's name).

Now, about those timing guides for cutting off caffeine, snacks, and drinks before snooze time! They're like your sleep guidelines. But remember, everyone's different. For instance, some people find they sleep better if they skip caffeine a whopping 8 hours before bedtime. And some people sleep soundly after a big glass of milk right before bed! It's all about finding what works best for you.

So, go ahead and try out different bedtime routines until you find your perfect sleep recipe!

Growing Pains & Marks

Growing pains and the ever-changing struggles of figuring out how long your legs are this month are common teenage stuff. Good food, drinks, and moving around can help you feel better. Sports and stretching can boost your coordination and confidence. I loved my dancing class in school—it made me feel good and helped me get used to my changing body. It's like a fun way to stretch, move, and find out what you're good at!

Stretch marks? Yeah, lots of us get them during those growth spurts. They happen when you grow fast or gain weight quickly. It's mostly about genetics, so no worries! Stretch marks and cellulite are just part of the deal as you grow up.

I shot up so fast during puberty that I went from a skinny kid to a more curvy grown-up shape in no time. Yep, I got stretch marks on my boobs, thighs, and butt. I used to hate them, but then I realized they're totally normal. Now, I see them as cool stripes, showing how much my body can change and grow.

If you want to try to avoid the appearance of stretch marks or cellulite, you can give your skin extra support. Use lotions, give yourself massages, and keep your skin hydrated and healthy. Try some Vitamin E treatments too—they might help!

Now, onto step 4 of this journey! How do you discover, fulfill, and balance your personal needs?

CHAPTER FOUR
DISCOVERING & BALANCING YOUR NEEDS

Wanting more independence while still craving a cozy place to belong? Figuring out what you need can be tricky, but we've got your back! Let's chat about your basic needs, how to live a happy and balanced life, and when to ask for support.

BUILDING ON YOUR NEEDS

As we move up the ladder of needs, we go from the basics like food and shelter to deeper stuff like safety, belonging, feeling good about ourselves, and reaching our full potential. And guess what? It's all easier when we're healthy, aware, have goals, and good people around us.

For me, the ultimate goal in life is to feel joyful and peaceful. Joy is like deep-down happiness that sticks around. It's about being present and intentional in our lives, living in a way that matches who we truly are. Joy isn't just something we stumble upon; it's something we create. That's why I chose my website CreatingOurJoy.com. Then, peace is all about feeling calm and balanced, no matter what's going on around us.

Finding joy and peace is a journey, and it's different for everyone. But there are things we can all do to get there, like practicing mindfulness, meditation, self-reflection, and keeping a positive outlook. It's all about finding what works for you and balancing work, fun, and rest. We'll dive deeper into this balance later on when we talk about the "wheel of life."

WORK & CAREER

Let's dive into the world of work and careers and how to start thinking about your future job path. Understanding the basics of career planning, business, and entrepreneurship can help you make smart choices about what's next. This means exploring different careers, seeing how they match up with your interests and skills, and planning your education accordingly. Education can come in all shapes and sizes, not just sitting in a classroom.

Here's a cool story about my brother after he graduated high school. Instead of jumping right into a job or college, he did something really neat. He did these mini-apprenticeships where he shadowed different people in all sorts of jobs for a few days. He found a welder, a butcher, a general contractor in home construction, and even a S.W.A.T. police officer! He got to see what different jobs were really like, and he even helped out on some projects. It was a great way for him to learn about himself and what he likes to do.

So, take some time to figure out what you're into. Try different things, see what gets you excited and what doesn't. Maybe you're into office work, or you prefer getting your hands dirty. Perhaps you like working solo, or you thrive in a team. And hey, you might even realize you want to start your own business or pursue something totally unconventional. The key is to explore and find what fits you best.

Tip & Action: *For you guys that want to hear more about my brother's experience and other amazing things he did that set him up for success as a teen and beyond: Stay updated on all my projects; make sure to visit my website, join my email list, or explore my Amazon author page. You can find QR codes and links at the very end of this book for quick reference.*

I've had the chance to explore different career paths, from nursing to corporate gigs to starting my own businesses. Each experience has been a journey of discovery, teaching me about myself and the world around me. When it comes to making a living, there are tons of options out there. Let's break them down into three main categories.

First, we've got university-based and white-collar jobs. These are the fancy-sounding ones like doctors, engineers, government workers, or big-shot managers. You hear a lot about these in school, and they're super important for keeping our society running smoothly. I've spent a lot of time in the corporate world, and I've really enjoyed the vibe and challenges there.

Then, there's the blue-collar and non-traditional jobs. These are the ones where you might get your hands dirty, like being a welder, plumber, or chef. You might not hear about these as much in school, but they're just as crucial for our communities. Plus, they can offer some serious independence and satisfaction.

Mike Rowe, the guy from "Dirty Jobs," is a big fan of blue-collar jobs. In a YouTube video called "TV Host Mike Rowe weighs in on Gen Z gravitating toward trade jobs" (CNBC Television, 2024), he talks about how lots of young folks are choosing trade jobs over going to university. Surprisingly, there are around 10 million of these jobs available right now, and you don't even need a four-year degree for most of them.

What you do need is some specific training or certifications, plus some on-the-job learning. But here's the cool part: these jobs can pay really well—often six figures a year! Plus, you save a ton of time and money by skipping the whole university thing. If you're interested, you can check out the Mike Rowe Works Foundation for more info and even some scholarships at mikeroweworks.org.

One of my closest pals works as a substation electrician for our local energy company. Seeing her grow in her job has been amazing. She's become so fulfilled, secure, and even wealthier because of it! Plus, she's picked up tons of handy skills like welding, electrical work, and plumbing, which come in handy both at work and at home.

Now, let's talk about the third group: the self-employed or business owners. These are the go-getters who run their own shows. Think small bake shop owners, freelance photographers, or even folks who own car mechanic shops. Being your own boss can be super rewarding, and there's a ton of potential to make big bucks and shape the economy.

Tip & Action: Need a hand with your financial game plan? Check out websites like thebalancemoney.com. They've got loads of helpful info on budgeting, investing, and career planning, perfect for young adults like you. Plus, they offer free aptitude tests, resume tips, and more to help you chart your path to success.

Resumes & Interviews

To ace either a job interview or pitch for your business, sharpening your skills is key. Whether you're seeking employment or hustling as an entrepreneur, nailing these techniques can boost your confidence and chances of success.

First up, the resume. Start with a good design, which you can easily find on Google Docs. Add your contact info, then highlight your value with a catchy intro. Next, list your work experience and any achievements. Break down your skills, and include your education and any other relevant sections.

Now, onto landing that interview. Research the job or deal you're after. What skills and experience do they want? What are the job duties listed on the posting? Once you're sure it's a good fit, tailor your resume accordingly. Then, prep for the interview based on the company's vibe and mission. Remember, every job and company is different, so adapt accordingly. Whether it's a small business or a big corporation, think about what they need from you to succeed in the role.

__Tip & Action:__ For top-notch career advice straight from a Human Resources and Recruiting Leader, check out the YouTube video "RUSHED Interview Prep - How to Prepare for a Job Interview at the LAST Minute!" by Self Made Millennial (2023). It's a goldmine of tips to get you ready for your next interview.

When it comes to selling, honesty, authenticity, and productivity are key. Whether you're pitching yourself or a product, these skills are super handy. You're always selling something, whether it's your skills, time, or energy, to employers, customers, friends, or potential partners.

The internet is bursting with tips and tricks, from mastering your posture to asking the right questions. Follow genuine and successful people on social media for specific advice. Test out different strategies and stick with what works best for you and your product.

__Tip & Action:__ And for those serious about honing their marketing skills, check out Alex Hormozi's $100M Leads System, available for free on acquisition.com/leads-gifts. It's a treasure trove of insights to level up your marketing game.

So, here is to you: discovering and developing your career skills! Don't let fear keep you from taking action; some opportunities only come once in a lifetime. Take courage, and take action!

HEALTH, BALANCE & WHEN TO GET HELP

When stuff in your life feels off, it can mess with your peace of mind and bring on stress and anxiety. That's why it's important to know what being healthy and safe means in all parts of your life. When you can spot what's healthy, you'll know when things aren't right and can steer clear. And if things get dangerous, you'll know when to reach out for support.

The Wheel of Life

A fun trick I use to check if my life is balanced is imagining it like a wheel. Each part of my life - like my spirituality, physical health, mental health, relationships, and freedom/money - is a spoke on that wheel. I give each area a rating to see how they're doing. Then, I imagine the different activities and levels of energy that need harmony and balance to keep me moving forward. I focus on work, play, and rest to keep my wheel rolling smoothly.

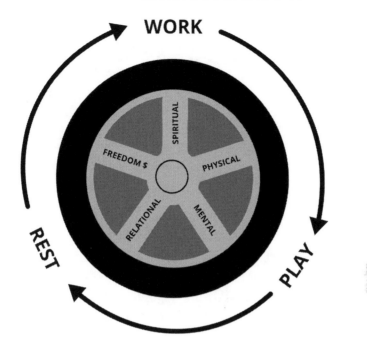

My family lives by a motto: "Read and Pray, Work and Play; these are things we do each day." It's been my guide through different times in my life. The main idea? Balance your energy in different parts of life. Just like a wheel needs, each spoke to be strong, and even, we need health and balance in every area. And remember, give the right time and space to work, play, and rest. How's each part of your life doing? Are they in harmony?

__Tip & Action:__ Think about your wheel of life. How is the strength of each spoke? Does it seem balanced? Is one lacking attention?

Now, think about the balance of your energy. How smooth and consistent is your motion forward? How is your work energy? Play and Rest? How are they balanced and working together?

What parts of your wheel of life could use a change and improvement?

Tip & Action: The incredible and life changing American author, coach, and speaker Tony Robbins has a similar analogy that I found later in life, you can use the Tony Robbins' Wheel of Life assessment to dive in deeper!

Mental & Emotional Health

In the book, The Whole-Brain Child (Siegel & Bryson, 2012), mental health is described as when all parts of the brain work well together. This means they integrate effectively, all online and working as they should. Mental and emotional health covers your psychological well-being, including your emotional and social wellness.

The World Health Organization's fact sheets on "Mental health" (2022), "Mental health is a state of mental well-being that enables people to cope with the stresses of life, realize their abilities, learn well and work well, and contribute to their community." Emotional health, meanwhile, is your ability to express feelings, adapt to emotional challenges, handle life's stresses, and find joy. It's like being emotionally literate so you can recognize, express, and manage your emotions.

During adolescence, your amygdala, the brain's emotion processor, is super active and under major construction, leading to intense feelings. Plus, you're dealing with a lot of first-time experiences – first love, loss, big wins, and letdowns. All this excitement can result in mood swings and emotional blowouts, but it's totally normal as your brain and life develop. Even when things feel like total chaos, give it time, be patient, and keep surrounding yourself with positivity – you'll get better at handling it.

When you feel overwhelmed or out of control, try recognizing it first. Then, switch things up by doing a new task or changing your environment, even if it's just in your mind. If you can, step outside or splash some water on your face. Personally, throwing ice cubes at a wall helps me blow off steam! Then, watching a ceiling fan spin helps calm my mind. Another trick is "bi-lateral stimulation," like tapping your feet alternately – it connects both sides of your brain and body, bringing back harmony.

Being aware of your emotions, like when and why you're feeling anxious, is super important for understanding yourself. Anxiety can come from feeling overwhelmed by options or your nervous system reacting to perceived threats. When you're anxious, ask yourself, "Am I safe right now?" If not, focus on getting to a safe place. If you are safe, thank your body for trying to protect you, then take steps to move forward.

Social anxiety is common as teens transition to independence. Finding comfort in yourself and spending time with supportive people can help ease it. Remember, it's okay to evolve and grow – different seasons of life bring different vibes and people who fill your cup (your soul's sense of safety, belonging, peace, and joy).

Self-awareness gives you power over your actions and reactions. If you know you get angry quickly, you can learn to manage it better. Strong emotions often stem from feeling our safety or standards are threatened. Instead of letting anger turn into rage or sadness into depression, focus on resolving issues and finding balance.

Being aware of and directing our internal self-talk in a positive way helps us see ourselves and the world in a healthier light. Our brain is like a supercomputer, absorbing all our experiences and using them to guide our thoughts and actions. So, when a negative thought pops up, like "I'm dumb" or "I'm a victim," I gently correct it. I might say, "That thing I did wasn't smart, but I'm brilliant and capable," or "I'm having a tough time, but I'll take steps to make it better." It's important to be kind to ourselves and choose positive thoughts to nourish our minds.

Tip & Action: For at least one day, pay attention to any negative thoughts that pop up automatically. When you notice them, replace them with more accurate, positive thoughts. You can say these replacements out loud or in your head. Consider jotting down these positive thoughts in a journal to reinforce them.

It's common to face mental health challenges, especially during adolescence. Recognizing these issues in yourself or your friends can be a big help. Depression, for instance, affects many teens and young adults. According to the Discovery Mood & Anxiety Program website (n.d.), "Suicide is the third-leading cause of death for young people ages 15 to 24. About 20 percent of all teens experience depression before they reach adulthood. Between 10 to 15 percent suffer from symptoms at any one time. Only 30 percent of depressed teens are being treated for it." Anxiety and eating disorders are also common in your age group, with helpful resources available from organizations like the National Eating Disorders Association.

When my close friend in high school confided in me that she had been cutting her inner thighs with a razor blade, it really caught me off guard. I felt a mix of shock, sadness, and confusion because she seemed almost proud of it. I didn't know how to respond or what to do at that moment.

It's important to remember that self-harm is often a sign that someone is struggling and in need of help. Looking back, I wish I had asked my friend more questions, like "Why are you doing that?" or "What feelings do you have before and after?" I would have also asked her how I could support her and how we could get her the help she needed. Those are the moments when it is vital to get help from trusted adults!

Knowing when and how to seek help is crucial. If you or someone you know is dealing with persistent feelings of sadness, anxiety, or disordered eating habits, reach out to trusted adults, parents/guardians, or a mental health professional. School counselors are often available to provide support or connect you with other resources in the community. Just like with physical health, finding a mental health professional you trust and feel comfortable with will make a big difference in getting the help you need.

Seeking help for mental health issues is incredibly brave, an act of courage, and very beneficial when done right! Resources like the National Alliance on Mental Illness (NAMI) Helpline can provide support, information, and local referrals. Find the resources for your area ahead of time, and save them on your phone if you can. When in doubt and needing immediate assistance, just dial your emergency number, 911 (999 in the UK), or go to your nearest emergency room, and they can direct you to the proper resources or send someone to help immediately.

<u>Tip & Action:</u> Refer again to the charts and details for "IF YOU OR SOMEONE YOU KNOW IS IN CRISIS OR STRUGGLING, HELP IS AVAILABLE" found in Chapter 1 > Section: Home Urgencies & Emergencies > subsection: Emergencies and Safety

Just as you can boost your physical health through diet and exercise, there are specific strategies to improve your mental and emotional well-being. These strategies might involve balancing different areas of your life and learning new skills through study and counseling.

Know that you are not alone; there are many beautiful people in this world that care so much about you. Many strangers who don't even know you feel so much love for the human race as a whole, and you are part of that! If you're reading this book, it's a sign that someone cares about you and wants to help. Whether someone gave you this book or you found it on your own, know that it's written out of love and with the intention of guiding and supporting you.

If you're dealing with physical, mental, or emotional challenges, don't hesitate to reach out to trusted adults and professionals for help. You deserve support and assistance on your journey to wellness!

Screen Time

Spending too much time on screens is a common issue that affects people of all ages. It's easy to get hooked on social media, games, or binge-watching shows, but excessive screen time can throw your life out of balance. This is especially important for young people whose brains are still developing.

We will dig more into dopamine and the reward system of your brain in Chapter 5 > Section: Learning & Studying. For now, understand, the adolescent brain is exceptionally responsive to the release of dopamine, a neurotransmitter associated with reward and pleasure.

Social media, in particular, is designed to keep us coming back for more. The likes, comments, and notifications trigger releases of dopamine and control our brain's reward system, making us crave that validation. But spending too much time online can take away from real-life experiences and relationships.

Using screens mindfully means being aware of how much time you spend online and taking breaks when needed. It's good and healthy to step away from screens and give your brain a rest. When we're constantly glued to our screens, we're not giving our brains a chance to grow and develop properly. So, remember to take breaks and give your brain a chance to thrive!

It's not uncommon for people to reach adulthood with an under-developed prefrontal cortex due to unhealthy screen habits, like mindless scrolling or consuming pornography. If you find yourself struggling with any addiction, whether it's to substances or behaviors, it's important to seek help.

The first step in overcoming any addiction is to accept that you can't do it alone and that you need support. Don't hesitate to reach out to trusted adults or professionals for help. They can provide guidance and support on your journey to recovery.

Technology and social media offer incredible opportunities for connection, growth, and learning, like never before in our known history. But just like anything else, they come with both benefits and risks. While technology can empower us, it can also become a source of addiction and distraction.

It's easy to get caught up in seeking instant gratification, which can lead to issues like depression and addiction. Plus, there are dangers like cyberbullying and privacy concerns to be aware of. That's why it's crucial to use digital tools responsibly, manage screen time, and prioritize online safety. By staying mindful of how we use technology, we can harness its benefits while minimizing its negative effects.

What you take into your body through your mouth, nose, and skin directly impacts your physical health. Likewise, what you take into your soul through your ears and eyes directly impacts your mental health. Just like living off a diet of fast food would be a recipe for physical disaster…

**Living off a shallow tech-based mental diet of
quick dopamine hits is a recipe for soul disaster.**

Setting limits on social media use, adjusting privacy settings, and being mindful of what you share online are all important steps for digital well-being. A friend of mine shared a great story about her son and his friends. They came together and decided to set goals and boundaries for their smartphone use. They passed their phones around in a circle, each setting screen time limits and passcodes to support each other in sticking to their goals. It's a fantastic example of how friends can help each other make positive choices and take responsibility for their digital habits.

Tip & Action: *Think about how you use technology. Do you seem to be more of a master of it and use it intentionally and as a tool, or does it often control and enslave you with its algorithms?*

If you feel like you want to improve your relationship with technology, think about what needs to be removed and what needs to be added in its place. Then follow my friend's example and ask for help from a friend or parent to set up screen time guides, or use an app like Opal: Screen Time for Focus.

After spending time on screens, it's essential to have a personal review. Reflect on how you felt during and after consuming certain content. Did it inspire you to connect with others and live a fuller life? Or did it leave you feeling sluggish and unmotivated, or even guilty or ashamed? Consider how you would feel if you shared what you saw with your loved ones.

Based on your reflections, be intentional about the content you engage with in the future. Use screens and the internet as tools for upliftment, education, connection, and motivation. By being mindful of the content you consume, you can cultivate a healthier digital lifestyle and promote your overall well-being.

Tip & Action: *Alright, it's time to really roll your sleeves up and follow the following prompts and questions!*

1. *Write down goals for how you want to feel during and after screen time.*
2. *What apps, content, and structure would produce that result?*
3. *Now, write down the content you often watch that doesn't produce the good/desired feelings and how it does make you feel.*
4. *What apps and content should you avoid or have limited time on to stop those negative side effects?*

My example: 1) I want to feel uplifted, connected, creative, and motivated when I have screen time. 2) I will use Instagram and Pinterest and will only follow specific people and content that produces those feelings and results. 3) I don't like the way I feel when I scroll through reels on YouTube, and I hate the way Snapchat makes my soul feel lost on its Discover page. 4) I won't scroll reels on YouTube and will only watch content I specifically search out & I will strictly only use SnapChat to message friends and use the "Hide This Content" a lot to help structure what shows up on my Discover page to avoid negative or click-bait content, if that doesn't work I will delete SnapChat.

You've got this! Answer all 4 questions! Then put in place what you need to in order to take the actions of steps 2) & 4)! ... Done? You are incredible, I imagine the percentage of people that are intentional and take action the way you just did is so rare today, you are a 1% already! I am so proud of you!!

Now, onto the skills keys that unlock doors to an even better internal landscape! Step 5...

CHAPTER FIVE

STEPPING INTO ACTION

I n this step, we'll explore what drives you, delving into the intricate workings of your thoughts and actions and embracing the powerful tool of self-awareness. We'll also delve into effective learning strategies, highlighting the importance of your social circle. Additionally, we'll discuss valuable goal-setting techniques to guide you on the journey toward your envisioned future adulthood.

SELF-AWARENESS

Understanding oneself is foundational for personal growth and development. It's akin to fixing a simple problem like replacing lead in a mechanical pencil—you need to grasp how it works and what it needs. Similarly, knowing our origins, how we function, and our needs is essential for functioning optimally in life. Understanding our family dynamics and upbringing provides insight into our behaviors and worldviews.

For example, growing up with a social butterfly mother would likely shape our social interactions and communication skills differently than if we had a homebody mother. By delving deeper into our past experiences and reflections, we uncover layers that inform our values and shape our narrative. This self-awareness enables us to navigate life authentically and align with our core values.

Tip & Action: *Think about some dynamics from your childhood. How have some shaped your current habits, priorities, or values?*

Understanding where you come from is like having a map for your journey through life—it helps you know yourself better. For instance, realizing you're awesome at hands-on learning but struggle with sitting still to read can guide how you study. You might find walking while listening to a story helps you learn better. Recognizing your strengths can boost your confidence and help you shine in areas you're naturally good at. When you know what you're good at, you can focus on those things and move forward faster!

Remembering or thinking about our past and how we've grown up can be tough sometimes. Maybe our memory isn't clear, or we've been through things that make us want to avoid thinking about it. It's important to seek help from a professional to work through tough stuff from the past. But we can also focus on who we are right now! Making a SWOT analysis can help with that. SWOT stands for Strengths, Weaknesses, Opportunities, and Threats. It's a way to list what we're good at, where we can improve, what chances we have, and what might stand in our way. It's a way to see our current selves clearly and plan for the future!

Tip & Action: *Create a list of at least ten things you are good at, things that leave you feeling energized and happy. You can ask for help to make this list. Look over the list and consider how to use your strengths and likes.*

Create a SWOT list and think about what may be standing in your way to achieving your goals.

Now, self-awareness helps you take charge of your life. It's about knowing what you want and making decisions based on that instead of just going along with what everyone else is doing. For example, if all your friends are vaping, but you know it's not right for you, being self-aware helps you say no confidently.

It's also about having your own opinions and ideas, not just repeating what you've heard from others. So, when you've done your own research and formed your own thoughts, you can listen to others respectfully, but still stick to what you believe in. Later on, we'll talk more about how to have great conversations and debates!

Self-awareness is knowing ourselves on an honest and deep level and understanding how others see us too. There are a lot of cool tricks we can use to boost our self-awareness. Mindfulness, journaling, self-reflection, personality awareness, and asking for feedback are the skills we will dive into here. Still, there is much more you can learn!

Ever tried the technique of mindfulness? It's like a secret sauce that helps you understand yourself better. It is done by tuning in to your thoughts and feelings without judging them; we instead welcome them with feelings of acceptance. We can use mindfulness to feel our emotions precisely as they are and pay specific attention to our physical sensations and surroundings.

Teenagers who practice mindfulness show increased self-awareness, control, calmness, and balance. Mindfulness also decreases a lot of the not-so-good stuff like anxiety, depression, physical pain, and distress or overwhelm. It is a powerful tool; with practice, you will be able to stay present and have more power over moments of anxiety, stress, intimidation, boredom, and depression.

Tip & Action: *To start, you can use YouTube to find channels and creators that offer good guidance, sounds, and vibes to match your desires. You can also look into apps like Headspace and Calm. Try searching on YouTube for "guided mindfulness exercises for beginners."*

Tip & Action: *Another fun mindfulness exercise to try is mindfully eating chocolate. For a step-by-step guide check out the article on PsychCentral "How to Practice Mindfulness with Chocolate" at psychcentral.com/blog/practicing-mindfulness-with-chocolate.*

Writing in a journal is like having your own secret hideout just for you. It's a spot where you can pour out all your thoughts and feelings. And get this: it's also a neat way for your future self or your family to learn more about you if you decide to share. I've checked out some journal entries from my ancestors, and it's wild how much it helps me understand them—and myself, too!

Keeping a journal is helpful for getting to know yourself better and dealing with stress. And guess what? There are a ton of cool ways to do it! You can list out things you're thankful for, jot down the best and worst parts of your day, or get artsy with photo collages and doodles. Seriously, there are no rules here, so you can go with whatever style sounds best to you!

Journaling can be simple, one of the most common ways I journal is to write out a short response to each of the following:

- List 3 things I am grateful for from today
- Write 1 highlight of the day
- Write 1 thing you would do different
- List the top 1 goal for tomorrow

I will have different prompts at different times or add more detailed things like:

- Write a story about what stood out to you today
- How would I act differently if you could do today again?
- Write the top 3 goals for tomorrow
- Write 1 way you can connect to a loved one

There are tons of ways to spice up your journaling! You can tailor it to whatever you're focusing on at the moment. Like, if you're aiming to journal every day, you can keep your prompts super easy-peasy. Or, if you're all about connecting with pals, throw in a prompt about reaching out to a friend each day. It's your journal, so you get to make the rules!

When we look back on our memories, it's like watching a movie with some scenes blurred out. But when we journal, it's like filling in those blurry parts with vivid details. You can start by writing down your thoughts and feelings for just a few minutes each day. As you keep at it, you'll notice patterns and learn more about yourself.

If you struggle to stick to paper journaling like me, you can try keeping an electronic journal instead. I find it super handy because I can make entries quickly, and it feels safe since my phone is always nearby and password-protected. Plus, using the speak-to-text feature makes it feel like I'm chatting with a friend about my day. If you have an iPhone, the Apple iOS system has a cool app called Journal that you might like!

Tip & Action: *When you start journaling, do it with the simple goal of (1) documenting what factually happened and (2) describing how you felt in those moments.*

Self-reflection is another skill for increasing self-awareness. It's like looking into a mirror for your mind. It helps you understand yourself better, make smarter choices, and handle your feelings. According to a study by Harvard Business Review "Why You Should Make Time for Self-Reflection (Even If You Hate Doing It)" (2017), it's said that "employees who spent 15 minutes at the end of the day reflecting about lessons learned performed 23% better after 10 days than those who did not reflect."

It's true! When you take time to think about your day, the things you did well, and what you could do better next time, you grow a lot. So, grab a journal, start small, and write down your thoughts in reflection of your day. Think about what went well, what didn't, and how you can do even better tomorrow.

Another big key to self-awareness is learning more about your personality type. Understanding your personality is like unlocking the secret code to yourself! It helps you see what you're really good at and where you might need a little extra help. There are lots of fun tests out there that can tell you more about your personality. They ask you questions about how you think, feel, and act and then give you cool insights into what makes you unique. Plus, it's super interesting to see how accurate they can be!

Tip & Action: *A couple of my favorite free personality tests are found on 16personalities.com/free-personality-test -or- kwikbrain.com/quiz; take a free personality test and review the insight provided.*

Asking for feedback from others is like unlocking a treasure chest of insights about yourself! It takes guts, but the rewards are huge, especially when you ask the right people. Sometimes, our friends and family can spot things about us that we might not see ourselves. So, reach out to those you trust and ask them about your strengths and weaknesses. Remember, the goal isn't to judge or criticize but to learn and grow. Approach the conversation with an open mind and a willingness to improve. Start by reflecting on your own thoughts, then chat with your trusted peeps and ask for their honest feedback on how you can become even better.

I like to handpick certain people and tap into their wisdom by asking for advice on specific areas where they excel. For example, if I'm aiming for financial success, I would seek guidance from someone who's really savvy with money. Likewise, if I want to improve my physical health, I'd turn to someone who's super fit and healthy. Asking for feedback and assistance might feel a bit scary, but it's actually super brave and essential for growing and improving. So, don't hesitate to reach out and learn from those around you!

Use your newfound self-awareness to set goals that really matter to you, taking into account your strengths, areas for growth, values, and beliefs. Make sure your goals reflect who you truly are. Your self-awareness can also help you improve your relationships. When you understand your emotions better, you can handle stress, recover from setbacks, communicate better, and build stronger connections with others. For example, if you notice that you often get defensive when someone criticizes you, you can practice listening more openly and responding in a more positive way.

Life holds constant change; you can't stop it. However, growing and learning from life is a choice you can make!

Self-awareness and discovery is a lifelong journey. With the changes and growth you experience, there is always more to learn about yourself and the world around you. Embrace the journey and enjoy the process of self-discovery. Recognize and celebrate the complexity and richness of your inner world.

LEARNING & STUDYING

Learning new things is like peeling layers off an onion – it's a process! First, get clear on what you want to learn and why. Ask yourself questions that intrigue you and set goals for what you want to achieve. Then, dive into the material and start understanding it bit by bit.

Once you've got a handle on a concept, share it with someone else. Teaching what you've learned to someone else helps reinforce your own understanding and strengthens your relationships. So, next time you discover something cool, share it with a friend or family member, or even post about it online!

A handy tool for exploring new topics is ChatGPT. You can ask ChatGPT to explain a subject and keep asking questions until you fully grasp it. For example, you could ask ChatGPT to break down a book like The Odyssey into simple points, one by one, and explain each one until you get it. This way, you can dive into subjects from school, hobbies, or anything else that catches your interest!

Dopamine Driven

Your teenage brain is like a sponge for dopamine, a chemical that makes you feel good. Our brains respond to it at a basic survival level; essentially, it is a drug we produce in our own brains that motivates us to act in certain ways. When we leverage it for our growth, it can supercharge our progress!

Dr. Andrew Huberman is an American neuroscientist, researcher, and podcaster who has done vast amounts of research and information sharing on dopamine and how to take advantage of the process. His work teaches great detail about dopamine and hope and how they help drive us in everything we do.

Tip & Action: *Visit his website, hubermanlab.com, and search terms like "dopamine" or "leverage dopamine." A great Podcast/video on his site is titled "Leverage Dopamine to Overcome Procrastination & Optimize Effort" from March 27, 2023.*

There is a dark side to dopamine to be aware of, too. Like how we touched on choosing intentional screen time, dopamine cycles can cause damaging effects and essentially turn us into dopamine drug addicts and can suppress our brain health and development if we don't take control over it! If you feel or recognize you are on the path of itching for dopamine hits from excessive actions or unhealthy activities, you should get help from your folks, friends, and even professionals.

Some examples of unhealthy dopamine-driven activities are:

- Social media scrolling: Spending excessive time on social media platforms, constantly scrolling, checking for likes, comments, and notifications, can lead to a dopamine loop and contribute to feelings of addiction and low self-esteem.

- Pornography consumption: Watching pornographic content can trigger a significant release of dopamine in the brain, leading to compulsive behavior and potential negative effects on relationships and mental health.

If you need help with porn consumption (in you or a partner), a helpful resource to check out is fightthenewdrug.org.

- Excessive video gaming: Engaging in long gaming sessions, especially with highly stimulating and addictive games, can lead to dopamine-driven behavior and neglect of other important aspects of life.
- Binge-watching TV shows or movies: Watching multiple episodes or movies in a single sitting can create a dopamine loop, where the pleasure of entertainment drives compulsive viewing behavior.
- Overeating junk food: Consuming foods high in sugar, salt, and unhealthy fats can lead to a surge in dopamine levels, contributing to overeating and potential health issues.

Back to the light side, when we use dopamine wisely, it can super-charge our learning and skill-building! Understanding how dopamine works can give you more control over your chosen paths. This awareness can also guide you to steer clear of harmful uses when coupled with unhealthy actions like extensive screen time. By knowing what motivates you, you can steer yourself toward positive growth and success and away from being controlled by it.

When you understand and lead your dopamine sources and responses, you can steer your own journey of learning and growth. This is a special time in your life when you can absorb information and skills like a champ! So, dive into different interests, try out new skills, and unleash your creativity. Whether it's learning a new language, jamming on a musical instrument, or mastering digital design, this is the perfect time to explore and conquer new horizons.

20 hours, New Skill

If you dedicate as little as 20 hours to a new skill, you can level up above most beginners. In an overview of Josh Kaufman's book "The First 20 Hours" (2013), he mentions, "By completing just 20 hours of focused, deliberate practice, you'll go from knowing absolutely nothing to performing noticeably well." If you divide that into 45-minute daily sessions, you can learn a new skill in one month!

Tip & Action: *Choose a new skill you want to become better at than a beginner, then make a plan. How will you have 20 hours of focused practice done on that skill in the next 6 months?*

Immersion Learning

Learning by immersion is like diving headfirst into a new adventure! Take Tony Robbins, for example. He's all about living your best life and inspiring others to do the same. One of his top tips for learning something new is diving in deep, like when you're learning a language. Instead of just studying a bit each day, immerse yourself fully!

Immersion learning can be super exciting and effective, especially when you fully dive into the experience. Let's say you're eager to learn Spanish. Instead of just sitting in a classroom day after day and not retaining much after a year... imagine going on a 10-day adventure into Mexico or Spain! Each day, you could spend four hours using language apps like Rosetta Stone or Duolingo to really get the basics down. Then, for the rest of the day, soak up the local culture and language by talking to people, exploring, and using tools like Google Translate to help you out. By the end of your trip, you'll have spent about 80 hours fully immersed in Spanish. It's like learning on steroids but way more fun!

Immersion learning can work even with a busy school schedule. Imagine taking a three-day weekend to dive headfirst into something to boost your productivity, like mastering speed reading, ace public speaking, or even learning how to code! It's all about that intense focus and dedication, and it's super effective for picking up new skills quickly. Plus, it's not just for school stuff – you can use it to become a pro at skateboarding, mastering guitar, or even whip up some amazing baked goods. This type of learning is known as "hyper fixation learning" and is common in the ADHD sphere. It really is a fantastic way to really develop new skills.

Whenever you are learning a new skill, adding guidance from experts is like adding a set of bumpers and a turbocharger to your progress. Let's say you're passionate about playing guitar. You could take advantage of a three-day break from school to dive deep into your learning. Imagine spending two hours each day in a guitar class, soaking up all the wisdom from your teacher. Then, you could use online resources like YouTube to keep practicing and honing your skills for another seven hours each day. That's a total of 20 hours of focused immersion learning in just three days – talk about turbocharging your progress! So, if you're looking to level up your skills, immersion learning is the way to go!

Tip & Action: *What is a new skill you could try learning by immersion? How could you do that? What master and mentor would you learn from?*

Academic Studies

Academics and studies are essential, but to do it effectively requires technique and balance. Each lesson is like a power-up for your brain, equipping you with the power to conquer problems, dissect equations, and outsmart tricky essays. Now, I get it, the call of Netflix and social media might be the Sirens tempting you away from your ship of studies. But hang tight because acing those topics helps unlock the universe's secrets, setting your course straight, one topic at a time.

Now, studying doesn't mean endless hours of boredom. It's all about working smarter, not harder. Ever heard of spaced repetition and active recall? These are like secret weapons for your study arsenal. Spaced repetition means having short review sessions over time to really nail down new info. And active recall? It's like using flashcards to quiz yourself on key concepts. With these techniques, you'll be studying like a pro in no time!

One study trick that really boosted my University game was recording myself going over the material. I'd break it down into questions with a pause for me to answer. Recording helped me organize and understand the info better. Then, I'd listen back to it while doing things like walking to school or during a quiet night shift. It was like having my own personal tutor on the go!

Time Slicing

I found this awesome trick to boost my productivity during study and work sessions! It taps into your brain's love for dopamine and its need for closure. Here's how it works: break your work into chunks with a timer, including focused work time and breaks. If you get interrupted, pause the timer and restart when you're back. When the timer rings, stop and take a break, even if you're mid-task.

This keeps you on a cliffhanger, eager for the next session, just like in your favorite TV show. Your brain craves closure, and this method uses that craving to keep you focused and motivated. Plus, regular breaks improve focus and memory. One popular technique is the Pomodoro Method: work 25 minutes, break 5, repeat 4 times, then take a 30-minute break.

Follow...

ACTION	WORK	BREAK	WORK	BREAK	WORK	BREAK	WORK	BREAK
TIME	25	5	25	5	25	5	25	30

... then **repeat** as long as available or needed

I tried out time-slicing for a recent project, but I found that 45-minute work sessions with 10-minute breaks worked even better for me. This technique can be super helpful, especially for folks with ADHD, because it breaks tasks into smaller, more manageable chunks. Remember, it's all about trial and error. Taking risks can lead to big rewards, so don't hesitate to experiment with different methods until you find what works best for you!

__Tip & Action:__ Figure out what learning styles, study and work methods, and time slices work best for you and your current tasks.

PLANS & GOALS

When planning your goals in life, it's essential to make them S.M.A.R.T. That means they should be Specific, Measurable, Achievable, Relevant, and Time-bound. For example, instead of saying, "I want to be good at drawing," you could say, "I will practice drawing for 30 minutes daily to prepare for the local art competition in six months." SMART goals give you clear direction and help you track your progress.

Let's take a general goal like "I want to get better at playing guitar" and make it SMART:

- Specific: "I will learn to play the song 'Wonderwall' by Oasis on the guitar."
- Measurable: "I will practice for 30 minutes every day."
- Achievable: "I will start by learning the basic chords and then progress to the more challenging parts of the song."
- Relevant: "Learning to play 'Wonderwall' aligns with my goal of improving my guitar skills and playing songs I enjoy."
- Time-bound: "I will be able to play 'Wonderwall' fluently within three months."

Now, let's talk about some common pitfalls to watch out for when setting goals and taking action. One big mistake is trying to tackle too many goals at once. This can overwhelm you and spread your energy too thin, making it harder to achieve any of them. Instead, focus on a few key goals at a time. This way, you can devote your full attention to them and feel more accomplished when you reach them. And remember, it's okay to say no to opportunities that don't align with your goals—it's all about staying focused and staying on track!

Implementing strengths in planning and goal-setting can turn your dreams into a roadmap for success. Just like planning a road trip, you begin with your starting point and map out your destinations along the way. Each checkpoint helps you appreciate how far you've come and keeps you on track. Planning isn't just about making daily to-do lists; it's about setting long-term goals, like getting into your dream college or landing a summer job. Good planning skills can also help beat procrastination by breaking tasks into smaller steps. And when you check off tasks, it boosts your confidence and keeps you motivated.

But planning isn't just about short-term tasks; it's also about creating a life plan. Your life plan isn't set in stone but evolves with your changing goals and interests. Start by figuring out your core values and passions, which will guide your long-term goals. For instance, if you love nature, your life plan might involve a career that lets you work outdoors, like helping to preserve wildlife or sharing the beauty of nature with others.

When working on your "Wheel of Life," it's crucial to first define long-term goals for each area. For example, in the aspect of a career, a long-term goal could be becoming a software developer. Then, shorter-term goals like learning a specific programming language within the year. Further breaking it down, a smaller goal could be adopting a study plan of 5 hours per week on specific material or scheduling immersive learning sessions.

Setting goals provides focus and motivation. Specific and SMART goals offer direction and purpose, acting as benchmarks for progress. Achieving small goals boosts confidence and motivates tackling larger challenges.

Remember, achieving goals is a journey. Celebrate progress, learn from mistakes, and keep moving forward. With a plan and goals, you have the power to shape your life!

__Tip & Action:__ Looking for more wisdom and guidance? Check out Dr. Jordan B. Peterson! While you may not agree with everything he says, his content sparks deep self-reflection and improvement. Explore his program on selfauthoring.com, designed to help you express your past, present, and future goals. Become the author of your own future with this valuable resource!

ASSOCIATION, FRIENDS & MENTORS

It's often said that you become like the people you spend the most time and energy with, so choose your company wisely and invest in them and yourself intentionally. Energy matters here because simply being around people isn't enough; you need to actively engage and build deeper relationships. Seek out mentorships, even if they're virtual, like tuning into inspiring podcasts and applying what you learn. Even a few hours a week can make a big difference in absorbing their wisdom.

To fast-track progress and shorten learning curves, surround yourself with people who have achieved the results you're after. This could mean joining a real-life group or finding virtual mentors who excel in different areas of life. For example, if you're into fitness, team up with gym buddies who are at or above your level. As a student, form a study group with classmates who share your academic goals. Together, you can leverage each other's strengths and knowledge to stay focused and motivated.

I had a fun study group in highschool where me and three other friends would spend about half our lunch breaks in the library studying, doing homework, and just chatting. This helped me to learn a lot, stay on track with my studies, and free up more after school time. I continued it in college too with different people!

Mentorship and accountability are key to reaching your goals. When planning your life and setting goals, seek guidance from mentors, trusted adults, or professionals like counselors or therapists. Don't hesitate to ask someone to mentor you or hold you accountable for your actions and progress.

When seeking a mentor, look for someone who's further along the path you want to take, someone you can learn from, and who is where you aim to be. Choose wisely, as you should pick up their habits and knowledge over time. For academic guidance, your older sister, who aced school with a 4.1 GPA, could be a great mentor, helping with study tips and time management.

When approaching someone to be your mentor, be clear about what you expect from them, even though some details may evolve over time. For instance, if you're asking a friend to mentor you in weightlifting, outline what that might involve, like working out together regularly and giving feedback on your progress. You can also hire professionals, like gym trainers or tutors, to mentor you in specific areas.

An accountability partner is someone you choose to help keep you on track and motivated. They don't need expertise in your field; they just need to be reliable and supportive. Be clear about your expectations when asking someone to be your accountability partner so they can decide if they're up for it.

For example, you could ask your little brother to be your accountability partner for your yoga routine. Let him know you'll be doing yoga every Monday, Wednesday, and Friday morning for 30 minutes, and ask him to remind you if you haven't started by 10 am.

If someone declines your request, don't stress; just find someone else. You can have different people as mentors and accountability partners. While other forms of accountability, like apps or reminders, can help, having a personal connection usually works best and can strengthen your relationship. You can also join groups with similar goals for mutual support and encouragement.

For added strength in your goal recipe, share your goals with trusted friends or family members! This can provide valuable support and encouragement. You can also offer to help them with their goals, creating a mutual accountability system. Whether it's through personal connections, apps (like Habitica or Strides), or other methods (like journaling or posting it on social media), having specific accountability measures increases your commitment to your goals.

As we journey through life and experience changes like puberty, it's crucial to adapt our goals to match our evolving selves. Surrounding ourselves with supportive people can make this process smoother and more fulfilling.

Now, let's explore what you will experience on your journey through the door of step number 6!

CHAPTER SIX

THE "INNER-PERSONAL" SOFT SKILLS

W hat does your internal landscape, soul, and mind feel like? Is it roaring waters, a river seemingly flowing the opposite way you want to go? Is it slow and stagnant? How can you differentiate between crippling overwhelm and motivating stress? How can you develop and use the skills we are about to discuss to guide your mind and the internal world to be more like a steady stream of clear waters?

TIME MANAGEMENT

Time management is like being the boss of your day! We all have 24 hours, no more, no less. It's the one thing we all share equally. So, how are you rockin' those hours? Are you balancing them well?

Time management isn't just about making a to-do list. It's about knowing how you use your time and making smart choices about it. Check out your phone's screen time or your YouTube watch history to see where your time goes. It's like peeking into your time habits!

Tip _&_ **_Action:_** _Check out how you have been using your screen time if you have a cellphone. If you have an iPhone, follow the steps; if you have another phone, or if iOS has updated to change the steps, figure it out for your phone..._

Go to your phone's [Settings], then [Screen Time], then [See All App & Website Activity]. Here, you can see your [Day] and switch to [Week] at the top.

This can help you have a realistic view of your Daily Average time on your phone screen and where that time is specifically used. Getting exact feedback like this will help keep you out of denial or avoidance.

Having a clear plan for each day can help you feel more in charge and less overwhelmed. A common and effective practice for scheduling is to do time blocks where you have a clear start and stop time for certain activities. Having a clear plan for each day can make life feel less crazy and more under control.

This can look like the 24-hour time chart here:

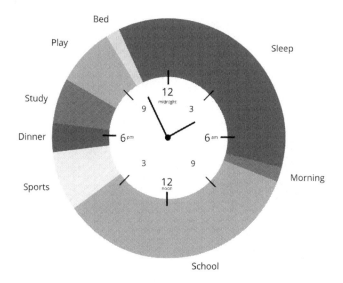

You can also try and use different tools that work best for you and your family, like Google Calendar. I have liked Google Calendar the best because you can create different calendars, colors, easily share it with your family, and update it on the go in real time. It helps me organize my entire life in one place!

Feeling overwhelmed with planning? Break down big tasks into smaller chunks. Let's say you've got a big project due soon. Plan out little steps to do each day, like brainstorming one day, getting supplies another, and so on.

And don't forget to balance things out! School and work are important, but so is fun! Schedule some chill time, even if just on weekends. And hey, don't skimp on rest and relaxation. Your brain and body need it to recharge!

STRESS & DISTRESS

Stress and overwhelm might seem similar, but they're actually different. Stress is a normal reaction to tough situations, like when our muscles ache and grow stronger after exercise. It can push us to do our best, like rushing to finish a project.

But sometimes, stress can turn into overwhelm or distress. This is when we feel like we can't handle everything and might even freak out. It happens when the pressure feels too much to handle. But don't worry, there are ways to deal with it!

To beat overwhelm, we can learn skills like organizing tasks, asking for help, and knowing when to say "no." It's important to avoid being overwhelmed because it can really mess with our minds and bodies. But with the right tools, we can keep stress in check and stay on top of things.

When you're feeling stuck and unsure what to do, focus on the things you can completely control. Like tidying up your room, staying hydrated, or applying for a few jobs. Some things, like where you live or if you'll get hired, are out of your hands for now. So start with what you can change!

Feeling decision and action paralysis?
Narrow down your actions to things that are in your complete control and start there!

When I am faced with a really big decision or scary situation, it helps me to think about the likely worst-case scenario. I recently found that it is actually a published psychological tool often called "decision-making under uncertainty" or "risk assessment."

Think of it like this: You know when you're trying to decide whether to do something, like maybe trying out for a sports team or asking someone out, but you're not sure what might happen? Well, this tool is like having a fortune teller that helps you imagine what could go really well (the likely best-case scenario) and what could go not-so-great (the likely worst-case scenario) if you make that choice. It's kind of like playing out different endings to a movie in your head before you decide what steps to take.

So first, I start by envisioning the likely worst-case scenarios. After I do that, I usually discover that it is something I can live with and that it isn't actually so bad. Then, I imagine my dream best-case scenario, which motivates me to take action. I use the combined "future fortunes" I just imagined and then figure out what action steps I need to take to avoid the worst and shoot for the best! So, by thinking about the possibilities, you can then make smarter decisions about what to do next!

When I feel overwhelmed, I take a breather and think about what really matters to me. Then, I move my body a bit, maybe do some stretches or go for a walk outside. Once I'm calmer, I rethink my plan and figure out what's most important. Sometimes, I realize I need to cut back on stuff that's stressing me out, like turning off the TV noise in the background, or taking a break from a podcast.

Here's a simple checklist I use to help me get back on track:

Feeling OVERWHELM or DISTRESS? Pause!

- Am I: thirsty, hungry, or tired?
  - If yes: How can I fix that now?
    - Do what you can now: drink, eat, go outside for some movement, take a nap?
- Is there excess: noise, stimulation, or worry?
  - If noise/stimulation: How can I fix that now?
    - Do what you can now: turn off the excess noise in the background?
  - If you have a worry: take a sticky-note(s) and write down what you are worrying about then either...
    - Fix it: If you can do something now.
    - Save it for later: If you need to do it at another time or with help, stick the note somewhere to remind you later.
    - Toss it out: If it is something you should not be worrying about or is out of your control, crumple up the note and throw it away. Do this while making a mental note to toss that worry out of your mind.

EMOTIONAL INTELLIGENCE

Emotional Intelligence (EI) is the ability to identify, understand, manage, and use emotions in positive ways. EI is as important as academic-related intelligence (IQ) for success in life. According to the Daniel Goleman website (n.d.), "Emotional intelligence refers to a different way of being smart. EI is a key to high performance, particularly for outstanding leadership. It's not your IQ, but rather it's how you manage yourself and your relationships with others."

Having high emotional intelligence (EI) is like having a supermind for your relationships. It helps you feel good, get along with others, and solve problems without drama. For example, instead of yelling at a friend who upset you, you could calmly tell them how you feel.

Emotional intelligence is useful everywhere, like at school, work, and with family and friends. In school, it helps with stuff like calming down before a test so you can do your best. At work, it makes you a great teammate because you understand how others feel. In family, friends, and partner relationships, it helps you talk about your feelings honestly and build trust.

To get better at EI, you can practice stuff like understanding your emotions, staying calm when things get tough, and learning from your experiences. And when you work on improving yourself, it can make everything else in your life better, too!

RESILIENCE & GROWTH MINDSET

As you make your plans, schedules, and decisions, remember that "failure" is just a stepping stone on the path to success. Think of Thomas Edison, who famously said he didn't fail 10,000 times trying to invent the lightbulb; he just found 10,000 ways that didn't work! Every setback is a chance to learn and grow.

The only real failure is giving up. As long as you keep trying, adjusting your plans, and taking action, you're still on the road to success. Remember, most goals take time and effort to achieve. If it were easy, it wouldn't be much of a challenge and would not help you grow, right?

Taking full responsibility for your life is key. Yes, you might have real and legit challenges or obstacles to overcome, like a tough family situation, physical health problems, or financial struggles. But focusing on what you can do — like your mindset and your actions — is where real change happens. So, keep pushing forward and never give up on your dreams!

If you haven't already, redefine "failure" in your mind to mean quitting. Then, understand that not succeeding at first is just part of the growth process. Changing how we see "failure" gives us a new perspective and helps us develop a powerful growth mindset.

The Psychologist Dr. Carol Dweck coined the term growth mindset. And in the article "Growth Mindset vs. Fixed Mindset: How what you think affects what you achieve" (Smith, 2020) we read "In Dr. Dweck's seminal work, she described the two main ways people think about intelligence or ability as having either:

- A fixed mindset: in this mindset, people believe that their intelligence is fixed and static.
- A growth mindset: in this mindset, people believe that intelligence and talents can be improved through effort and learning."

Having a growth mindset means believing we can become smarter through effort, goals, and time. This belief, along with our efforts, directly leads to higher achievement levels and greater success and resilience.

Resilience is the ability to bounce back from setbacks and keep going in the face of challenges. It helps us turn roadblocks into stepping stones. For example, if you didn't make the school soccer team, you can use the setback as motivation to train harder or pivot and find a different sport you enjoy more.

Building resilience involves developing a positive mindset and viewing challenges as opportunities for learning. Overcoming procrastination and staying motivated are key to achieving goals. Strategies like optimizing dopamine drive and using the Pomodoro Technique can help maintain focus and productivity. Visual reminders of goals, like pictures of your dream destination, can also keep you motivated. Creating a vision or dream board is another helpful tool to stay focused and inspired.

**Tip & Action:** _You can use apps like Be Focused-Focus Timer, or other habit and timer apps, to help you overcome procrastination and take action._

Don't forget to celebrate your small wins along the way! These victories keep you motivated and build momentum toward your goals. While it's important to focus on your ultimate destination, don't overlook the beauty and satisfaction of your journey. Take a moment to appreciate how far you've come from where you started and the joy in each step of your progress.

Practice mindfulness and gratitude for the present moment and your current successes. Reflect on the things you're experiencing now that you once wished for in the past. While it's essential to plan for the future, prioritize gratitude for the present and take action toward your goals.

Now, we have covered a lot of ways you can improve your inner world! So, let's get ready to bring it all together and figure out how you can apply those skills and more to have better relationships with other people and the world around you! Onto our last steps in chapter 7!

CHAPTER SEVEN
THE "INTER-PERSONAL" SOFT SKILLS

I t's totally okay if you're not sure what you want in life right now. Sometimes it's easier to think about what we don't want instead. And hey, that's a great place to start! Knowing what we don't want can help us figure out how to steer clear of it and head towards something better.

When it comes to relationships and other people, it's kind of like knowing which "rooms" we don't want to be in. Once we figure that out, we can make a beeline for the door and find our way into healthier, happier spaces. So take some time to learn and think about what you don't want, and then use that to guide you towards what you do want. You've got this!

RELATIONSHIPS & COMMUNICATION

Healthy Relationships

Understanding healthy relationships is super important so you know what's good for you, what you need to work through, and what you should steer clear of. All healthy relationships share some key stuff: respect, honesty, being real, caring, talking things out, and feeling safe.

Sometimes, though, we end up in not-so-healthy relationships. Often, it's not our choice, like with family. Other times, we pick the wrong people or things just go sour. But here's the deal: You always deserve to feel safe and have a say in your choices. Knowing what abuse is can help you spot it and figure out how to get help if you need it.

Abuse comes in lots of forms, and sometimes, it's hard to see it for what it is, especially if it's all you've ever known. It could be physical, like hitting or pushing, messing with your mental health or your tech devices, or controlling your money. If you're in a tough spot, there are hotlines you can call any time of day for support and advice.

Tip & Action: The organization Women Against Abuse has resources that outline how abuse may present itself in a relationship. If you want to learn more, go to [womenagainstabuse.org] and look at the [Education] section and the [Learn about Abuse] subsection. There are resources about [Teen Dating Violence], [Types of Abuse] and more.

You can also find support on mind.org.uk, the article " Guide to support options for abuse" has good guides and resources.

Communication Skills

Improving how we talk to others, and even to ourselves, is a cool skill to work on! Being humble and open to hearing other people's thoughts is a good way to start. Also, learning to really listen, understand how others feel, and sort out conflicts can make chats way smoother and friendships way stronger.

When you're talking, keeping it clear and simple is key. Use words everyone can get, and try to match your tone and body language to what you're saying. Think about it like being a character in a story: Would you rather chat with Tigger and Pooh or Eeyore? Enthusiasm and curiosity can make conversations way more fun and interesting!

Now, if you're into telling stories or cracking jokes, there are some tricks to make them pop! First, start with something catchy, keep things moving along, and save the big moment for just the right time. Plus, paint a picture with your words so people can really see what you're saying. It's like being a stand-up comedian or a master storyteller! Practice, watch the pros, and see how your audience reacts. Then, tweak and try again!

Conversation Blueprints

Learning to be a good listener can totally take your relationships to the next level! It's like being an empty cup, ready to be filled with a refreshing drink poured in by someone else. Sure, it might take some practice and patience to be open and steady, but trust me, it's totally worth it!

First off, when someone's talking to you, try to really understand what they're saying. Repeat it back to them in a way to make sure you've got it right. And hey, before you jump in with your own thoughts, ask if they want your input. It shows you respect their point of view and want to hear them out.

Active listening is all about making the other person feel heard and valued. So, instead of worrying about what you're gonna say next or how you'll come across, focus on what they're saying and where they're coming from. It's like putting on their glasses for a sec to see things their way.

Active Listening Blueprint

- **ACTIVE LISTENING** to the other person, working to understand their perspective.
- **CHECK FOR UNDERSTANDING** by repeating key points and telling them what you think they mean.
- If your understanding was off, repeat active listening.
- **ARE YOU OPEN TO FEEDBACK?** Is something to ask once you agree you understand what they are telling you.
- **WHAT DO YOU WANT?** Is another question to ask how you can support them.
- **CAN I RESPOND?** Is a question to ask when you want a turn to discuss what you are thinking and want to communicate.

  - If so, proceed with your thoughts and feelings in a respectful, honest, and true way.

When you're sharing your thoughts and feelings, stick to what actually happened and how it made you feel. Avoid assuming their intentions or blaming them with extreme statements like "you always" or "you meant to hurt my feelings." Instead, focus on your own emotions and experiences. Keep going back and forth until you both feel understood or decide to take a break.

S.E.W. Method

A handy method for handling tough talks comes from Julie Colwell Ph.D. in her book The Relationship Skills Workbook. It's called S.E.W., which stands for Sensations, Emotions, and Wants. This method helps you express your own experiences clearly and directly. By focusing on what you feel and need, it keeps everyone grounded in the present moment. You can find a summary of this method in the article "S.E.W.-ing your way out of power struggle" (Colwell, 2017).

It is key to keep your communication based on facts and what actually happened or is happening to avoid arguments. To communicate your experience and needs to someone else in a way that is unarguable, you can follow her blueprint:

First start with **your bodily SENSATIONS**, by telling someone exactly what you are physically feeling. This could be things like a tightening in your chest, fluttering in your stomach, hotness on your neck, shivering in your core, or energized spine.

Then, you tell them what **EMOTIONS you are feeling** in connection with those sensations. The main emotions to identify from the sensation are sad, mad/angry, scared/fearful, glad/happy/loving, and excited/surprised/aroused.

Lastly, you tell them **what you WANT**, or don't want, to happen as a result of your experienced feelings and emotions. This could be something like "I want to spend more time with you", "I want help to clean the kitchen", or "I don't want to go to xyz place".

For example, you could be really frustrated by the way you perceive someone is interrogating you or won't leave you alone. You would express yourself like the following...

"I feel hotness in my face and neck, and I feel a tightness in my stomach. I am feeling mad and sad. I want to have some alone time right now."

When we're in situations where we can't get what we want, like during a family road trip or when our parents ask lots of questions to ensure our safety, staying grounded in our bodies can help. It lets us communicate what's going on inside us and express our needs clearly. If we can't get exactly what we want, we can try negotiating or finding another solution. For example, if you want alone time but can't have it right away since you are stuck in the car with your family, you could say, "I want everyone to give me space and let me listen to calming music with my eyes closed."

Steps to the S.E.W. Method

- Sensations: communicate what bodily sensations you are feeling.
- Emotions: are you feeling... sad, angry, fearful, happy, excited?
- Wants: what do you want or not want to happen?

Tip & Action: For more on this method visit Dr. Colwell's website addresses at *juliacolwell.com/archives/3401 & juliacolwell.com/archives/2036*.

Ground Rules

These skills and blueprints work best when both people are on the same page and put in equal effort to be respectful and follow the plan. Practice with your family or friends might feel awkward at first, but it helps the pattern stick and ensures everyone knows what to expect in future conversations or conflicts.

If you're actively listening and need to share your feelings, but you're not ready, or the other person isn't listening well, it's okay to call a time-out. This means pausing the conversation and suggesting to continue it later when it can be more productive. Whoever calls the time-out should say when the conversation will pick up again. For example, if things get tense talking with your mom about school, you could say, "Hey, I don't think we're getting anywhere right now. Let's take a break and talk again tomorrow at 4:00."

Conflict resolution skills are super important for keeping relationships healthy. We all have disagreements, but how we deal with them makes a big difference. Imagine arguing with your sibling about chores at home. Instead of pointing fingers, try using the blueprint we talked about earlier to understand each other's points of view and find a fair solution together.

Having tough conversations can be uncomfortable at first, but it's worth it. As you practice, it gets easier, and you'll see that real relationships thrive when you can talk about anything, even the hard stuff. This goes for your relationship with yourself, too.

Take time to explore your thoughts and feelings, and surround yourself with people who are open to deep conversations. Life is richer when we dive into what really matters, and having those close connections reminds us that we're never alone.

Honesty

Honesty is like the glue that holds relationships together. It's all about being straightforward and not hiding things. If someone asks you something and you're not comfortable sharing, it's okay to say so. For example, if your friend invites you to the movies, but you're already hanging out with someone else she doesn't like, don't make up an excuse. Just tell her the truth: "I'd love to go see that movie with you but can't make it tonight, but how about next Tuesday or Friday?" That way, you're being honest and respectful of both your friends.

Being honest is where it all begins in any relationship, including the one you have with yourself. Take a good look inside, and be willing to see both your strengths and weaknesses. Trying to convince yourself of something false only wastes your time and energy. Your body and brain know the truth, even if you'd rather ignore it. Being honest about your actions, desires, and dislikes is essential. When you're transparent with yourself, you create room for growth and understanding, paving the way for a better life.

Learning to understand and listen to your gut and intuition while being aware of your surroundings is important for safety. Awareness of who is a known and safe person, how to tell if someone is unsafe, and what to do if someone makes you feel "icky" is vital.

I first always strive for complete honesty, with good boundaries, in my safe relationships. Then, I remember the importance of learning/remembering how to lie well to protect myself from strangers and unsafe people.

Know who you can trust and how to spot someone who might not be safe. If someone gives you a bad feeling, it's okay to lie for your safety. For example, if a stranger in a store asks if you live nearby, you can say you're just visiting family and your dad is outside waiting for you. And if you ever feel uncomfortable or unsafe, don't hesitate to ask for help! In a store, you could pretend you forgot something and ask an employee to walk you to your car. Your safety comes first!

Understanding honesty also involves knowing the differences between surprises, holding confidence, and keeping a secret. A surprise is something kept hidden temporarily, bringing happiness when revealed, like a Christmas gift. Holding confidence means safeguarding private information like your friend telling you she peed her pants on her way home last week, but she doesn't want you to tell anyone else. Maybe a friend is dealing with a medical condition she is getting help for but doesn't want other people to know about. If keeping their confidence won't cause harm, it's crucial to respect their trust and keep it to yourself.

Then there are secrets. A clear way to understand secrets is to see them as things you intentionally keep hidden, especially if they're unhealthy or harmful. Discuss this with your guardians, but as a minor, you should learn not to keep secrets from safe adults. While many things are kept private among responsible adults, secrets should never involve pain, abuse, or harm. It's important to have open communication with trusted adults to ensure your safety and well-being.

Understanding these principles is crucial for your safety and well-being. If you've been told to keep something a secret from your trusted parents or guardians in the past, it's important to tell them and seek professional help if needed. If you have promised to keep a secret in the past, and you break that promise now by telling the safe adults in your life, know that you are doing the right thing. You can always break a "promise" to seek or provide safety.

Tip & Action: *Discuss with your parents/guardians the value of honesty and their guidance on secret-keeping and lying. Roleplay different scenarios with them, like how to respond to strangers probing for information or how to respond when a friend asks you to keep an unhealthy secret.*

Tip & Action: *For more guidance on the crucial relationship skills of honesty, compassion, empathy, authenticity, and vulnerability, see the works of Brene Brown, namely The Power of Vulnerability.*

Boundaries & Bonuses

All healthy relationships require good boundaries. Boundaries are not just lines you draw in the sand; they are beautiful fence lines that protect our sacred spaces and selves. Mastering the art of saying no is not just a skill, it's a key to your success and the implementation of healthy boundaries. If saying no feels challenging, remember that you're not just declining one thing, you're actually opening the door to so much more in return.

Internal boundaries are like the rules we set for ourselves when we're alone or with others. For example, deciding to exercise every Saturday morning is a way of saying yes to good health and no to sleeping past 9 am. Internal boundaries are important to help promote self-respect and safety.

External boundaries, on the other hand, are the limits we establish with other people. They determine how we expect to be treated in relationships, what conversations and topics are okay around us, and the behaviors we're comfortable with. When we respect these boundaries, our relationships become healthier, and our environment becomes more positive.

<u>Boundaries:</u> THEY DO NOT change or control other people; THEY DO help filter standards and people into and out of our lives.

<u>Tip & Action:</u> Think of actions and interactions you have experienced recently that make you uncomfortable. Think of actions you took or interactions you have had with others. Ask for help from guardians and friends as needed. What kind of boundaries could you put in place to help create a space of more peace, safety, and respect for yourself?

Boundaries are not legit unless they come with consequences. Sometimes, these consequences happen naturally, like feeling tired and slow if you skip your Saturday morning workout. But other times, we need to set consequences ourselves and let others know about them. For example, you might say to your friend Joe, "If you keep interrupting me, I won't continue this conversation." Or to your roommate Sally, "If you don't wash the dishes you use, we'll have to keep our dishes separate." And to your brother John, "If you borrow my car and don't return it clean and with a full tank, you won't be able to borrow it again."

Consequences aren't about controlling others; they're about keeping ourselves safe and respected. Like, if you keep crossing your own boundary of screen time use, then you need to implement the consequence of having your folks or friends set up parental time blocks. When someone crosses our boundaries, consequences give us time to feel safe again and create barriers to prevent it from happening too often.

Tip & Action: Take the boundaries you thought of a moment ago and figure out some consequences that go with them. These could be natural and automatic consequences or ones you plan to implement if the boundaries are violated. If there are consequences you would need to implement, think of how you would do that with yourself or when involving others.

Bonus: Understanding attachment styles is super helpful because they affect how we connect with others. There are three main attachment styles: secure, anxious, and avoidant. Your attachment style mostly comes from your experiences in childhood. But the good news is, you can learn skills to have a healthier attachment style and work through tough experiences to become more secure in your relationships.

Tip & Action: To learn more about your attachment style, or the style of those around you, you can dive into the book Attached and take the online quiz at attachedthebook.com.

Bonus: Understanding love languages is like having a secret code to show love to the people we care about. There are five types: physical touch, words of affirmation, quality time, gift-giving, and acts of service. Knowing which love language someone speaks helps us show love in a way that really clicks for them. For example, if your mom loves acts of service, doing chores around the house could make her day. And if your sister is into gifts, surprising her with a little something can go a long way. When we speak each other's love languages, it's like filling up each other's love tanks and making each other feel super special. Plus, it saves us from wasting time, energy, and money on things that don't really hit the spot.

Tip & Action: *You can find more information and guidance on that in the book The Five Love Languages by Gary Chapman or on the website 5lovelanguages.com.*

Leadership & Team Skills

Good teamwork is like a puzzle where everyone has a piece to fit. In teams, there are leaders and supporters, just like in an army or sports team. The best leaders are like coaches—they guide and help their teammates shine. If you want to learn about leadership, check out folks like George Washington, Mahatma Gandhi, Winston Churchill, Martin Luther King Jr., Steve Jobs, Michael Jordan, and Elon Musk to see what qualities you admire.

Leaders lead by example, showing their team how to work hard and stay motivated. They're also great problem-solvers, spotting issues before they become big problems. But being a leader isn't just about telling people what to do. It's also about trusting your team and giving them the tools and freedom to do their jobs well.

Delegation is a big part of leadership. It means assigning tasks to team members based on their strengths. Good leaders give clear instructions and check in regularly to make sure everything's on track. And while leaders might take on extra tasks, they also know when to share the workload.

In a team project, the leader helps organize and divide tasks, making sure everyone has something to do. They might take on extra work or help smooth things out when the project comes together. Being a leader isn't always easy, but it's a great way to learn and grow while helping your team succeed. Plus, in life, it usually literally pays off because it results in a higher income, better project outcomes, and a greater rate of learning and application of diverse skills.

Debate & Public Speaking

Debate and discourse are essential for understanding and problem-solving, whether in school, work, or life. Here are some tips for making your discussions more effective:

1. Research and prepare thoroughly to understand both sides of the argument and gather evidence to support your position.
2. Structure your argument with a clear introduction, main points, and conclusion.
3. Use analogies and persuasive language to make your points compelling.
4. Be clear and concise in your communication to ensure your points are understood.
5. Stay calm and respectful, avoiding personal attacks.
6. Actively listen to understand the argument and counterpoints effectively.
7. Stay open-minded and willing to change your position based on new information.
8. Participate actively in discussions by asking questions and contributing meaningfully.
9. Stay informed about various perspectives and facts to enrich your contributions.
10. Respect differences and foster inclusivity by validating others' experiences and viewpoints.
11. Use boundaries and consequences to maintain peace in heated conversations.

12. Aim for solutions or consensus rather than just debating for the sake of argument.

Public speaking skills are also crucial and can be developed alongside debate skills. Here are some tips for effective public speaking:

1. Know your audience and tailor your message to resonate with them.
2. Organize your content with a clear structure and engaging opening.
3. Use supportive examples and evidence to illustrate your key ideas.
4. Pay attention to body language and voice control to engage the audience.
5. Control nervousness by practicing deep breathing and using stress to stay focused.
6. Use techniques like looking above the crowd or blurring the audience to manage nervousness.
7. Record and review your practice to improve your delivery and confidence.
8. Study other speakers, like studying the way someone speaks in a recorded TED Talk or lecture.

By honing your debate and public speaking skills, you can become a more effective communicator and problem solver in various aspects of your life.

ONLINE SKILLS

When you're chatting online, it's like entering different worlds, each with its own rules! Imagine you're at a big party: how you talk with your buddies might be super casual, but if you're talking with a teacher or boss, you'd use your more serious voice, right? Same goes for social media and emails!

So, on Snapchat, X, or TikTok, you can let loose with emojis and slang, but if you're emailing your teacher or applying for a job, it's time to bring out the formal language and ditch the emojis. It's like wearing the right outfit for the occasion! Just remember to match your message to the platform and audience.

If you need help to format something in a more professional way you can plug the following into ChatGPT... Take what I paste below and format it into a professional email for me to send to my boss/administrator.

Now, online relationships can open up a whole new world of possibilities, but it's important to stay safe out there! If you ever encounter cyberbullying or grooming or feel uncomfortable online, don't hesitate to speak up. Tell a trusted adult or report it to the social media platform and, in severe cases, to the local authorities.

When you're chatting online, it's like navigating through a digital jungle. Be careful not to share personal info and watch out for red flags. And hey, ever heard of 'netiquette'? It's like having good manners but for the internet! Respect others, double-check before you share, and keep your digital footprint tidy.

Websites like cybercivics.com offer resources to learn about netiquette. Knowing how to protect yourself online is essential in the digital age. This includes creating strong passwords, recognizing phishing attempts, and managing your digital footprint. Resources like staysafeonline.org provide tips for internet safety.

Here are some savvy tips to keep you safe in the digital world:

1. Trust Your Gut: If it feels fishy, it probably is! Don't fall for anything that sounds too good to be true.
2. Know the Scams: From phishing emails to fake websites, be on the lookout for common scams lurking online.
3. Stay Skeptical: Don't trust messages or calls from unknown sources. Scammers love to slide into your inbox uninvited!
4. Watch Out for Phishing: Be extra cautious of emails or messages that ask for personal info or urge you to click on suspicious links.
5. Check Those URLs: Before clicking away, make sure the website's URL looks legit. Watch out for sneaky misspellings or odd characters!
6. Verify the Sender: Double-check the identity of anyone contacting you online. Legit folks won't rush you into making decisions.
7. Lock Down Your Passwords: Keep your accounts safe with strong, unique passwords. Don't make it easy for hackers to swoop in!
8. Keep It Hush-Hush: Be stingy with your personal deets online. Scammers love to scoop up info for their sneaky schemes.
9. Don't Let Them Pressure You: Slow down and think twice before acting on urgent messages. Scammers use time-sensitive tricks to panic you!
10. Do Your Homework: Before buying or sharing anything online, snoop around for reviews and feedback. It's like Yelp for the digital world!
11. Charity Check: Make sure your donations are going to the right place by verifying charities before giving. Better safe than sorry!

12. Update Your Defenses: Keep your security software up-to-date to ward off online baddies. It's like giving your digital fortress a shiny new coat of armor!

13. Stay Stealthy: Protect your info with incognito mode and a VPN when surfing the web. It's like slipping on an invisibility cloak for your data!

14. Be Wary in Public: Be extra cautious when using personal devices on public Wi-Fi. Don't let hackers crash your online party!

15. Speak Up: If you spot anything shady online, don't be shy! Report it to someone you trust, like a parent or teacher.

Stay sharp, stay safe, and enjoy your online adventures responsibly!

MAKE A DIFFERENCE FOR OTHER TEENS WITH YOUR REVIEW

If you enjoyed this book, and haven't already, please help others and leave an honest and favorable review through Amazon.

To get those 'feel good vibes' and help some people for real, all you have to do is take one minute and…**leave a review.**

Simply scan the QR code below,
then leave a review!

* Bonus Level * attach a photo to your review! Maybe your favorite page or a shot of the _**Tip & Action**_ you want to try next.

CONCLUSION

Well, here we are, at the close of these life skills for teens; it's not the end, though! I call on you to review the sections and information that speaks to you at this time in your life. Do the **_Tip & Action_** items that resonated with you most. Then, return again and again in the future and review the book!

**Tip & Action:** A good way to review and work through this book would be to return to the table of contents and make a list or mark the chapter sections you want to work on first. Then go through each section and subsection one at a time and work on understanding more and improving the related skills!

This could look like marking Chapter 7 to start with Relationships & Communication. Then deciding you want to start with the subsections of Boundaries & Bonuses, then the S.E.W. Method. Then, for this week you dive deeper into the Boundaries details, then next week the S.E.W. Method. Then you keep going!

Stay updated on all my projects; make sure to visit my website, join my email list, or explore my Amazon author page. You can find QR codes and links at the very end of this book for quick reference.

I'm thrilled to have been a part of your learning journey! Taking the time to dive into this book is just the beginning of all the amazing things you'll accomplish. Your dedication to self-improvement is truly inspiring.

Remember to keep your goals in sight and never stop striving for your dreams. With each step you take, you're getting closer to the life you envision. And don't forget to share your journey with those you love—they'll be your biggest supporters along the way!

Keep shining bright and chasing after your dreams. I believe in you!

One of your biggest cheerleaders! - Joy Pack

REFERENCES

Why You Should Make Time for Self-Reflection — Even If You Hate Doing It. (2017, March 20). Harvard Business Review. https://hbr.org/2017/03/why-you-should-make-time-for-self-reflection-even-if-you-hate-doing-it.

The First 20 Hours. (2013). Retrieved from https://first20hours.com/#:

NIH, National Library of Medicine. (2010). Adolescent Changes in the Homeostatic and Circadian Regulation of Sleep. Retrieved from https://www.ncbi.nlm.nih.gov/pmc/articles/PMC2820578/.

CNBC Television. (2024, April 2). TV Host Mike Rowe weighs in on Gen Z gravitating toward trade jobs [Video]. YouTube. https://www.youtube.com/watch?v=9k3ShxE2VOw.

Self Made Millennial. (2023). RUSHED Interview Prep - How to Prepare for a Job Interview at the LAST Minute! [Video]. YouTube. https://www.youtube.com/watch?v=UFSQwVFRLtM&t=30s.

Siegel, D. J., & Bryson, T. P. H. D. (2012). *The Whole-Brain Child.* Random House.

World Health Organization. (2022, June 17). Mental health. *WHO.* Retrieved from https://www.who.int/news-room/fact-sheets/detail/mental-health-strengthening-our-response.

Discovery Mood & Anxiety Program. (n.d.). Today's Teens Are More Depressed Than Ever. Retrieved from https://discoverymood.com/blog/todays-teens-depressed-ever/#:

Daniel Goleman. (n.d.). Emotional intelligence refers to a... Retrieved from https://www.danielgoleman.info/#:

Smith, J. (2020, September 25). Growth Mindset vs Fixed Mindset: How what you think affects what you achieve. *Mindset Health.* https://www.mindsethealth.com/matter/growth-vs-fixed-mindset.

Colwell, J. (2017). S.E.W.-ing your way out of power struggle. *Julia B. Colwell, Ph.D. Personal Transformation through Relationship.* Retrieved from. https://juliacolwell.com/archives/2036.

Gautam, V. (2023, September 4). *Albert Einstein Called Compound Interest 'Eighth Wonder Of The World' And It's True. Here's Why. IndiaTimes.* Retrieved from https://www.indiatimes.com/worth/news/albert-einstein-compound-interest-eighth-wonder-of-the-world-614000.html.

Duley, M. (2023, March 27). *Here's How Much Americans Are Saving in 2023 vs. 2022.*

GoBankingRates. Retrieved from https://www.gobankingrates.com/money/how-do-americans-savings-stack-up-in-2023-vs-2022/.

Internal Revenue Service. (n.d.). Publication 554: Tax Guide for Seniors. IRS. Retrieved from https://www.irs.gov/publications/p554#:

Centers for Disease Control and Prevention (CDC). (n.d.). Creating and Storing an Emergency Water Supply. Retrieved from https://www.cdc.gov/healthywater/emergency/creating-storing-emergency-water-supply.html#:

NYC Department of Health and Mental Hygiene. (n.d.). Whole Foods. NYC Health. https://www.nyc.gov/site/doh/health/health-topics/whole-foods.page.

EWG (Environmental Working Group). EWG'S Shopper's Guide to Pesticides in ProduceTM. (2024). Retrieved from https://www.ewg.org/foodnews/full-list.php.

Chris Fleming. (2015). COMPANY IS COMING [Video]. Youtube. https://www.youtube.com/watch?v=GBwELzvnrQg&t=48s.

Peacock. (2023). Zero-tolerance Phil is a monster [Video]. YouTube. https://www.youtube.com/watch?v=ighhAKWgd_s.

The Office. (2023). Fire Drill - The Office US [Video]. YouTube. https://www.youtube.com/watch?v=gO8N3L_aERg.

Modern Family Clips. (2020). Modern Family 1x16 - Haley takes her driver's test [Video]. YouTube. https://www.youtube.com/watch?v=wOztuj6nGk8.

Here are the QR codes I will refer to throughout the book to my website CreatingOurJoy.com & my Amazon author page

MY WEBSITE

MY AMAZON

CreatingOurJoy.com

Author Site

Made in the USA
Columbia, SC
23 October 2024

44921358R00100